Teaching Mathematics in the
Visible Learning Classroom
Grades 6–8

Teaching Mathematics in the Visible Learning Classroom

Grades 6–8

John Almarode, Douglas Fisher,
Joseph Assof, Sara Delano Moore,
John Hattie, and Nancy Frey

CORWIN **Mathematics**

FOR INFORMATION:

Corwin

A SAGE Company

2455 Teller Road

Thousand Oaks, California 91320

(800) 233-9936

www.corwin.com

SAGE Publications Ltd.

1 Oliver's Yard

55 City Road

London EC1Y 1SP

United Kingdom

SAGE Publications India Pvt. Ltd.

B 1/I 1 Mohan Cooperative Industrial Area

Mathura Road, New Delhi 110 044

India

SAGE Publications Asia-Pacific Pte Ltd

18 Cross Street #10-10/11/12

China Square Central

Singapore 048423

Executive Editor, Mathematics: Erin Null

Editorial Development Manager: Julie Nemer

Editorial Assistant: Jessica Vidal

Production Editor: Tori Mirsadjadi

Copy Editor: Christina West

Typesetter: C&M Digitals (P) Ltd.

Proofreader: Scott Oney

Indexer: Will Ragsdale

Cover and Interior Designer: Rose Storey

Marketing Manager: Margaret O'Connor

Printed in the United States of America.

Library of Congress Cataloging-in-Publication Data

Names: Almarode, John, author.

Title: Teaching mathematics in the visible learning classroom, grades 6-8 / John Almarode [and five others].

Description: Thousand Oaks, California : Corwin, a Sage company, [2019] | Includes bibliographical references and index.

Identifiers: LCCN 2018032570 | ISBN 9781544333182 (pbk. : alk. paper)

Subjects: LCSH: Mathematics teachers—In-service training. | Mathematics—Study and teaching (Elementary) | Mathematics— Study and teaching (Middle school)

Classification: LCC QA10.5 .T434 2019 | DDC 510.71—dc23 LC record available at https://lccn.loc.gov/2018032570

This book is printed on acid-free paper.

19 20 21 22 10 9 8 7 6 5 4 3

Contents

List of Videos

Introduction

Video 1: What Is Visible Learning for Mathematics?

Video 2: Creating Assessment-Capable Visible Learners

Chapter 1. Teaching With Clarity in Mathematics

Video 3: What Does Teacher Clarity Mean in Middle School Mathematics?

Chapter 2. Teaching for the Application of Concepts and Thinking Skills

Video 4: Learning Intentions in an Application Lesson

Video 5: Finding the Right Application Task

Video 6: Differentiating in an Application Lesson

Video 7: Facilitating and Evaluating Learning in an Application Lesson

Video 8: Consolidating Deep and Transfer Learning in an Application Lesson

Chapter 3. Teaching for Conceptual Understanding

Video 9: Aligning a Conceptual Task to the Learning Intention

Chapter 4. Teaching for Procedural Knowledge and Fluency

Video 10: Differentiating Instruction to Support Surface, Deep, and Transfer Learning

Note From the Publisher: The authors have provided video and web content throughout the book that is available to you through QR (quick response) codes. To read a QR code, you must have a smartphone or tablet with a camera. We recommend that you download a QR code reader app that is made specifically for your phone or tablet brand.

online resources

Videos may also be accessed at resources.corwin.com/ vlmathematics-6-8

Acknowledgments

We are forever grateful for the teachers and instructional leaders who strive each day to make an impact in the lives of learners. Their dedication to teaching and learning is evident in the video clips linked to the QR codes in this book. The teachers at Health Sciences High & Middle College have graciously opened their classrooms and conversations to us, allowing us to make mathematics in the Visible Learning classroom evident to readers. Louisa County Public Schools did the same. The learners they work with in the Louisa County Public Schools are better simply because they spent time with the following people:

Ms. Caroline Brooks, Louisa County Middle School

Ms. Rachel Green, Louisa County Middle School

Ms. Ashley Lewis, Louisa County Middle School

Mr. Jesse Cleaver, Louisa County High School

Mr. William Patrick, Louisa County High School

Dr. Lisa Chen, Assistant Superintendent for Instruction

We are extremely grateful to Superintendent Doug Straley for allowing us into the schools and classrooms of Louisa County, helping to make our work come alive.

Ms. Ashley Norris is an excellent teacher in Columbia County Public Schools in Georgia. She is actively engaged in implementing Visible Learning in her mathematics classroom. Her contributions to Chapter 5 provide a clear example of how she has taken the Visible Learning research and translated the findings into her teaching and learning. We are forever grateful to her for sharing her journey with us so that we could share these examples with you.

About the Authors

John Almarode, PhD, has worked with schools, classrooms, and teachers all over the world. John began his career in Augusta County, Virginia, teaching mathematics and science to a wide range of students. In addition to spending his time in PreK–12 schools and classrooms, he is an associate professor in the Department of Early, Elementary, and Reading Education and the codirector of James Madison University's Center for STEM Education and Outreach. In 2015, John was named the Sarah Miller Luck Endowed Professor of Education. However, what really sustains John—and what marks his greatest accomplishment—is his family. John lives in Waynesboro, Virginia, with his wife, Danielle, a fellow educator; their two children, Tessa and Jackson; and their Labrador retrievers, Angel and Forest. John can be reached at www.johnalmarode.com.

Douglas Fisher, PhD, is Professor of Educational Leadership at San Diego State University and a teacher leader at Health Sciences High & Middle College. He is the recipient of a William S. Grey Citation of Merit and NCTE's Farmer Award for Excellence in Writing, as well as a Christa McAuliffe Award for Excellence in Teacher Education. Doug can be reached at dfisher@mail.sdsu.edu.

Joseph Assof is an 11th- and 12th-grade mathematics teacher and the math department chair at Health Sciences High & Middle College in San Diego, California. He leads his department's reform efforts to align to the Common Core Standards—with a focus on high-quality instruction. He is a member of the San Diego County Math Leaders Task Force, whose mission is to support every student in meeting the rigorous expectations of the Common Core. Joseph's classroom is featured in a number of *Visible Learning for Mathematics, Grades K–12* videos.

Sara Delano Moore, PhD, is Director of Professional Learning at ORIGO Education. A fourth-generation educator, her work focuses on helping teachers and students understand mathematics as a coherent and connected discipline through the power of deep understanding and multiple representations for learning. Sara has worked as a classroom teacher of mathematics and science in the elementary and middle grades, a mathematics teacher educator, Director of the Center for Middle School Academic Achievement for the Commonwealth of Kentucky, and Director of Mathematics & Science at ETA hand2mind. Her journal articles appear in *Mathematics Teaching in the Middle School, Teaching Children Mathematics, Science & Children*, and *Science Scope*.

John Hattie, PhD, has been Laureate Professor of Education and Director of the Melbourne Education Research Institute at the University of Melbourne, Australia, since March 2011. He was previously Professor of Education at the University of Auckland, as well as in North Carolina, Western Australia, and New England. His research interests are based on applying measurement models to education problems. He has been president of the International Test Commission, has served as adviser to various ministers, chairs the Australian Institute for Teachers and School Leaders, and in the 2011 Queen's Birthday awards was made "Order of Merit for New Zealand" for his services to education. He is a cricket umpire and coach, enjoys being a dad to his young men, is besotted with his dogs, and moved with his wife as she attained a promotion to Melbourne. Learn more about his research at www.corwin .com/visiblelearning.

Nancy Frey, PhD, is Professor of Literacy in the Department of Educational Leadership at San Diego State University. She is the recipient of the 2008 Early Career Achievement Award from the National Reading Conference, and she is also a teacher leader at Health Sciences High & Middle College and a credentialed special educator, reading specialist, and administrator in California.

Introduction

Please allow us to introduce you to Ashley Norris, Joanna Halstrom, Luciana Fernandez, and Jasvinder Singh. These four middle school mathematics teachers set out each day to deliberately, intentionally, and purposefully impact the learning of their students. Whether they teach sixth, seventh, or eighth grade, they recognize that

- They have the capacity to select and implement various teaching and learning strategies that enhance their adolescent learners in mathematics;

- The decisions they make about their teaching have an impact on their students' learning;

- Each and every student can learn mathematics and they take responsibility to teach *all* learners in their middle school mathematics classes; and

- They must continuously question and monitor the impact of their teaching on student learning. (adapted from Hattie & Zierer, 2018)

Through the videos accompanying this book, you will meet three additional middle school mathematics teachers and the instructional leaders that support them in their teaching. Collectively, the recognitions above—or their **mindframes**—lead to action in their mathematics classrooms and their actions lead to outcomes in student learning. This is where we begin our journey through *Teaching Mathematics in the Visible Learning Classroom*.

Visible Learning occurs when teachers *see* learning through the eyes of their students and students *see* themselves as their own teachers. How do teachers of mathematics see integers, rational numbers, absolute

> **Mindframes** are ways of thinking about teaching and learning. Teachers who possess certain ways of thinking have major impacts on student learning.

1

value, proportional relationships, functions, and linear equations through the eyes of their students? In turn, how do teachers develop assessment-capable visible learners—students who see themselves as their own teachers—in the study of numbers, operations, and relationships? Conceptualizing, implementing, and sustaining Visible Learning in the middle school mathematics classroom by identifying *what works best* and *what works best when* is exactly what we set out to do in this book.

Mathematics learning involves the balance of conceptual understanding, procedural knowledge, and the application of concepts and thinking skills to a variety of mathematical contexts. By balance, we mean that no one dimension of mathematics learning is more important than the other two. Conceptual understanding, procedural knowledge, and the application of concepts and thinking skills are each essential aspects of learning mathematics. Mathematics classrooms where *teachers see learning through the eyes of their learners and learners see themselves as their own teachers* result from specific, intentional, and purposeful decisions about each of these dimensions of mathematics instruction critical for student growth and achievement. This book explores each of these components in middle school mathematics teaching and learning through the lens of *what works best* in student learning at the surface, deep, and transfer phases. We are not suggesting that teachers implement procedural knowledge, conceptual understanding, and application in isolation, but through a series of linked learning experiences and challenging mathematical tasks that result in students engaging in both mathematical content and processes.

Our **Learning Intention**: To understand what works best in the middle school mathematics classroom.

What Works Best

Identifying what works best draws from the key findings from Visible Learning (Hattie, 2009) and also guides the classrooms described in this book. One of those key findings is that *there is no one way to teach mathematics or one best instructional strategy that works in all situations for all students*, but there is compelling evidence for certain strategies and approaches that have a greater likelihood of helping students reach their learning goals. In this book, we use the effect size information that John Hattie has collected and analyzed over many years to inform how we transform the findings from the Visible Learning research into learning experiences and challenging mathematical tasks that are most likely to have the strongest influence on student learning.

For readers less familiar with Visible Learning, we would like to take a moment to review what we mean by *what works best*. The Visible Learning database is composed of over 1,800 meta-analyses of studies that include over 80,000 studies and 300 million students. Some have argued that it is the largest educational research database amassed to date. To make sense of so much data, John Hattie focused his work on meta-analyses. A **meta-analysis** is a statistical tool for combining findings from different studies, with the goal of identifying patterns that can inform practice. In other words, a meta-analysis is a study of studies. The mathematical tool that aggregates the information is an effect size, and can be represented by Cohen's *d*. An **effect size** is the magnitude, or relative size, of a given effect. Effect size information helps readers understand not only that something does or does not have an influence on learning but also the relative impact of that influence.

For example, imagine a hypothetical study in which learning mathematics while sitting on a stability ball results in relatively higher mathematics scores. Schools and classrooms around the country might devote large monetary resources to removing traditional chairs and desks, replacing this furniture with stability balls for all of the middle school mathematics classrooms. However, let's say the results of this hypothetical study also indicate that the "stability ball effect" had an effect size of 0.03 in mathematics achievement over the control group, an effect size pretty close to zero. Furthermore, the large number of students participating in the study made it almost certain there would be a difference in the two groups of students (those using a stability ball versus those not using a stability ball). As an administrator or teacher, would you still advocate for spending large amounts of your district or school budget on non-traditional seating? How confident would you be in the impact or influence of your decision on mathematics achievement in your district or school?

This is where an effect size of 0.03 for the "stability ball effect" is helpful. Understanding the effect size helps us know how powerful a given influence is in changing achievement—in other words, the impact for the effort or return on the investment. The effect size helps us understand

A **meta-analysis** is a statistical tool for combining findings from different studies, with the goal of identifying patterns that can inform practice.

Effect size represents the magnitude of the impact that a given approach has.

Video 1
What Is Visible Learning for Mathematics?

To read a QR code, you must have a smartphone or tablet with a camera. We recommend that you download a QR code reader app that is made specifically for your phone or tablet brand. Videos can also be accessed at *https://resources.corwin.com/ vlmathematics-6-8* not just what works, but *what works best*. With the increased frequency and intensity of mathematics initiatives, programs, and packaged curricula, deciphering where to best invest resources and time to achieve the greatest learning outcomes for all students is challenging and frustrating. For example, some programs or packaged curricula are hard to implement and have very little impact on student learning, whereas others are easy to implement but still have limited influence on student growth and achievement in mathematics. Teaching mathematics in the Visible Learning classroom involves searching for those things that have the greatest impact and produce the greatest gains in learning, some of which will be harder to implement and some of which will be easier to implement.

As we begin planning for our first period Math 6 class or our afternoon Math 8 class, knowing the effect size of different influences, strategies, actions, and approaches to teaching and learning proves helpful in deciding where to devote our planning time and resources. Is a particular approach (e.g., classroom discussion, exit tickets, use of calculators, a jigsaw activity, computer-assisted instruction, simulation creation, cooperative learning, instructional technology, presentation of clear success criteria, development of a rubric, etc.) worth the effort for the desired learning outcomes of that day, week, or unit? With the average effect size across all influences measuring 0.40, John Hattie was able to demonstrate that influences, strategies, actions, and approaches with an effect size greater than 0.40 allow students to learn at an appropriate rate, meaning at least a year of growth for a year in school. Effect sizes greater than 0.40 mean more than a year of growth for a year in school. Figure I.1 provides a visual representation of the range of effect sizes calculated in the Visible Learning research.

Before this level was established, teachers and researchers did not have a way to determine an acceptable threshold, and thus we continued to use weak practices, often supported by studies with statistically significant findings.

Consider the following examples. First, let us consider classroom discussion. Should teachers devote resources and time to planning for the facilitation of classroom discussion? Will this approach to mathematics provide a return on investment, rather than "chalk talk" where we work out lots of problems on the board for students to include in their notes?

EFFECT SIZE FOR
ABILITY GROUPING
= 0.12

THE BAROMETER OF INFLUENCE

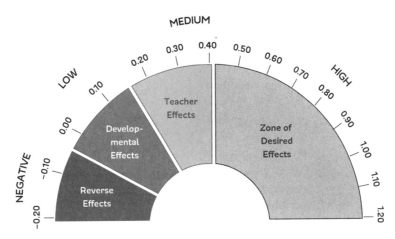

Source: Hattie, J. (2009). *Visible learning: A synthesis of over 800 meta-analyses relating to achievement.* Figure 2.4, page 19. New York, NY: Routledge.

Figure I.1

With classroom discussion, teachers intentionally design and purposefully plan for learners to talk with their peers about specific problems or approaches to problems (e.g., demonstrating multiple representations of operations with fractions or comparing and contrasting dependent and independent events) in collaborative groups. Peer groups might engage in working to solve complex problems or tasks (e.g., determining congruence or graphing inequalities on a number line). The students would not be **ability grouped**, but rather grouped by the teacher to ensure that there is academic diversity in each group as well as language support and varying degrees of interest and motivation. As can be seen in the barometer in Figure I.2, the effect size of classroom discussion is 0.82, which is well above our threshold and is likely to accelerate learning gains.

Therefore, individuals teaching mathematics in the Visible Learning classroom would use classroom discussion to understand mathematics learning through the eyes of their students and for students to see themselves as their own mathematics teachers.

Ability grouping, also referred to as tracking or streaming, is the long-term grouping or tracking of learners based on their ability. This is different from flexibly grouping students to work on a specific concept, skill, or application or address a misconception.

THE BAROMETER FOR THE INFLUENCE OF CLASSROOM DISCUSSION

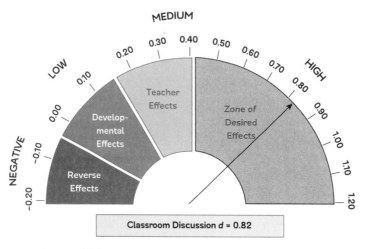

Source: Adapted from Hattie, J. (2009). *Visible learning: A synthesis of over 800 meta-analyses relating to achievement.* Figure 2.4, page 19. New York, NY: Routledge.

Figure I.2

EFFECT SIZE
FOR CLASSROOM
DISCUSSION = **0.82**

EFFECT SIZE
OF USE OF
CALCULATORS
= **0.27**

Second, let us look at the use of calculators. Within academic circles, teacher workrooms, school hallways, and classrooms, there have been many conversations about the use of the calculator in mathematics. There have been many efforts to reduce the reliance on calculators while at the same time developing technology-enhanced items on assessments in mathematics. Using a barometer as a visual representation of effect sizes, we see that the use of calculators has an overall effect size of 0.27. The barometer for the use of calculators is shown in Figure I.3.

As you can see, the effect size of 0.27 is below the zone of desired effects of 0.40. The evidence suggests that the impact of the use of calculators on mathematics achievement is low. However, closer examination of the five meta-analyses and the 222 studies that produced an overall effect size of 0.27 reveals a deeper story to the use of calculators. Calculators are most effective when they are used (1) for computation, deliberate practice, or learners checking their work; (2) to reduce the amount of cognitive load on learners as they engage in problem

THE BAROMETER FOR THE INFLUENCE OF USING CALCULATORS

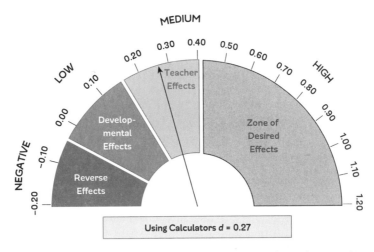

Source: Adapted from Hattie, J. (2009). *Visible learning: A synthesis of over 800 meta-analyses relating to achievement.* Figure 2.4, page 19. New York, NY: Routledge.

Figure I.3

solving; and (3) when there is an intention behind using them (e.g., solving by graphing or approximation problems). This leads us into a second key finding from John Hattie's Visible Learning research: *We should not hold any influence, instructional strategy, action, or approach to teaching and learning in higher esteem than students' learning.*

What Works Best When

Visible learning in the mathematics classroom is a continual evaluation of our impact on student learning. From the above example, the use of calculators is not really the issue and should not be our focus. Instead, our focus should be on the intended learning outcomes for that day and how calculators support that learning. Visible Learning is more than a checklist of dos and don'ts. Rather than checking influences with high effect sizes off the list and scratching out influences with low effect sizes, we should match the *best* strategy, action, or approach with learning needs of our students. In other words, is use of calculators the right strategy

Teaching Takeaway

Using the right approach at the right time increases our impact on student learning in the mathematics classroom.

or approach for the learners at the right time, for this specific content? Clarity about the learning intention brings into focus what the learning is for the day, why students are learning about this particular piece of content and process, and how we *and* our learners will know they have learned the content. Teaching mathematics in the Visible Learning classroom is not about a specific strategy, but a location in the learning process.

Over the next several chapters, we will show how to support mathematics learners in their pursuit of conceptual understanding, procedural knowledge, and application of concepts and thinking skills through the lens of *what works best when*. This requires us, as mathematics teachers, to be clear in our planning and preparation for each learning experience and challenging mathematics tasks. Using the guiding questions in Figure I.5 (on pages 12–13), we will model how to blend what works best with what works best *when*. You can use Figure I.5 in your own planning. This planning guide is found also in Appendix B and online at **resources.corwin .com/vlmathematics-6-8**.

EFFECT SIZE FOR
ASSESSMENT-
CAPABLE VISIBLE
LEARNERS = **1.33**

Through these specific, intentional, and purposeful decisions in our mathematics instruction, we pave the way for helping learners see themselves as their own teachers, thus making them assessment-capable visible learners in mathematics.

The Path to Assessment-Capable Visible Learners in Mathematics

Teaching mathematics in the Visible Learning classroom builds and supports assessment-capable visible learners (Frey, Hattie, & Fisher, 2018). With an effect size of 1.33, providing a mathematics learning environment that allows learners to see themselves as their own teacher is essential in today's classrooms.

Assessment-capable visible mathematics learners are

1. Active in their mathematics learning. Learners deliberately and intentionally engage in learning mathematics content and processes by asking themselves questions, monitoring their own learning, and taking the reins of their learning. They know their current level of learning.

An assessment-capable visible learner says, "I am comfortable finding the area of a circle but need more learning on surface area and volume. I know there are examples in my interactive notebook that I can use to prepare for tomorrow's challenge problem."

2. Able to plan the immediate next steps in their mathematics learning within a given unit of study or topic. Because of the active role taken by an assessment-capable visible mathematics learner, these students can plan their next steps and select the right tools (e.g., manipulatives, problem-solving approaches, and/or meta-cognitive strategies) to guide their learning. They know what additional tools they need to successfully move forward in a task or topic.

An assessment-capable visible learner says, "To find the volume of this cylinder, I am going to calculate the radius of the circle rather than measure it. This makes my volume calculation more precise."

3. Aware of the purpose of the assessment and feedback provided by peers and the teacher. Whether the assessment is informal, formal, formative, or summative, assessment-capable visible mathematics learners have a firm understanding of the information behind each assessment and the feedback exchanged in the classroom. Put differently, these learners not only seek feedback but also recognize that errors are opportunities for learning, monitor their progress, and adjust their learning. (adapted from Frey et al., 2018)

Video 2
Creating Assessment-Capable Visible Learners

https://resources.corwin.com/vlmathematics-6-8

An assessment-capable visible learner says, "Yesterday's exit ticket surprised me. Ms. Norris wrote on my paper that I needed to revisit the process for isolating the unknown variable. So, today, I am going to work out the entire process in my notebook and not try and do it all in my head."

Over the next several chapters, we will explore how to create a classroom environment that focuses on learning and provides the best environment for developing assessment-capable visible mathematics learners who can engage in the mathematical habits of mind represented in one form or another in every standards document. Such learners can

1. Make sense of problems and persevere in solving them.
2. Reason abstractly and quantitatively.
3. Construct viable arguments and critique the reasoning of others.

ASSESSMENT-CAPABLE VISIBLE LEARNERS

ASSESSMENT-CAPABLE LEARNERS:

 KNOW THEIR CURRENT LEVEL OF UNDERSTANDING

 KNOW WHERE THEY'RE GOING AND ARE CONFIDENT TO TAKE ON THE CHALLENGE

 SELECT TOOLS TO GUIDE THEIR LEARNING

 SEEK FEEDBACK AND RECOGNIZE THAT ERRORS ARE OPPORTUNITIES TO LEARN

 MONITOR THEIR PROGRESS AND ADJUST THEIR LEARNING

 RECOGNIZE THEIR LEARNING AND TEACH OTHERS

Source: Adapted from Frey, Hattie, & Fisher (2018).

Figure I.4

4. Model with mathematics.

5. Use appropriate tools strategically.

6. Attend to precision.

7. Look for and make use of structure.

8. Look for and express regularity in repeated reasoning (© Copyright 2010. National Governors Association Center for Best Practices and Council of Chief State School Officers. All rights reserved.).

How This Book Works

As authors, we assume you have read *Visible Learning for Mathematics* (Hattie, Fisher, Frey, Gojak, Moore, & Mellman, 2017), so we are not going to recount all of the information contained in that book. Rather, we are going to dive deeper into aspects of middle school mathematics instruction that are critical for students' success, helping you to envision what a Visible Learning mathematics classroom like yours looks like. In each chapter, we profile three middle school teachers who have worked to make mathematics learning visible for their students and have influenced learning in significant ways. Each chapter will do the following:

1. Provide effect sizes for specific influences, strategies, actions, and approaches to teaching and learning.

2. Provide support for specific strategies and approaches to teaching mathematics.

3. Incorporate content-specific examples from middle school mathematics curricula.

4. Highlight aspects of assessment-capable visible learners.

Through the eyes of sixth, seventh, and eighth grade mathematics teachers, as well as the additional middle school mathematics teachers and the instructional leaders in the accompanying videos, we aim to show you the mix and match of strategies you can use to orchestrate your lessons in order to help your students build their conceptual understanding, procedural fluency, and application of concepts and thinking

HOW TO USE APPENDIX B WHEN PLANNING FOR CLARITY

I have to be clear about what content and practice or process standards I am using to plan for clarity. Am I using only mathematics standards or am I integrating other content standards (e.g., writing, reading, or science)?

Rather than what I want my students to be doing, this question focuses on the learning. What do the standards say my students should learn? The answer to this question generates the **learning intentions** for this particular content.

Once I have clear learning intentions, I must decide when and how to communicate them with my learners. Where does it best fit in the instructional block to introduce the day's learning intentions? Am I going to use guiding questions?

As I gather evidence about my students' learning progress, I need to establish what they should know, understand, and be able to do that would demonstrate to me that they have learned the content. This list of evidence generates the **success criteria** for the learning.

ESTABLISHING PURPOSE

1 What are the key content standards I will focus on in this lesson?

Content Standards:

2 What are the learning intentions (the goal and *why* of learning, stated in student-friendly language) I will focus on in this lesson?

Content:

Language:

Social:

3 When will I introduce and reinforce the learning intention(s) so that students understand it, see the relevance, connect it to previous learning, and can clearly communicate it themselves?

SUCCESS CRITERIA

4 What evidence shows that students have mastered the learning intention(s)? What criteria will I use?

I can statements:

online resources — This planning guide is available for download at resources.corwin.com/vlmathematics-6-8.

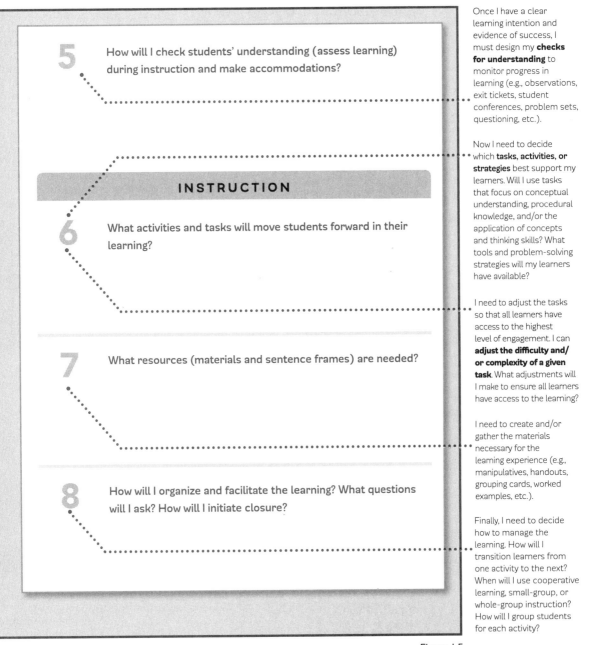

5 How will I check students' understanding (assess learning) during instruction and make accommodations?

Once I have a clear learning intention and evidence of success, I must design my **checks for understanding** to monitor progress in learning (e.g., observations, exit tickets, student conferences, problem sets, questioning, etc.).

INSTRUCTION

6 What activities and tasks will move students forward in their learning?

Now I need to decide which **tasks, activities, or strategies** best support my learners. Will I use tasks that focus on conceptual understanding, procedural knowledge, and/or the application of concepts and thinking skills? What tools and problem-solving strategies will my learners have available?

7 What resources (materials and sentence frames) are needed?

I need to adjust the tasks so that all learners have access to the highest level of engagement. I can **adjust the difficulty and/ or complexity of a given task**. What adjustments will I make to ensure all learners have access to the learning?

I need to create and/or gather the materials necessary for the learning experience (e.g., manipulatives, handouts, grouping cards, worked examples, etc.).

8 How will I organize and facilitate the learning? What questions will I ask? How will I initiate closure?

Finally, I need to decide how to manage the learning. How will I transition learners from one activity to the next? When will I use cooperative learning, small-group, or whole-group instruction? How will I group students for each activity?

Figure I.5

skills in the most visible ways possible—visible to you and to them. If you're a mathematics specialist, mathematics coordinator, or methods instructor, you may be interested in exploring the vertical progression of these content areas PreK–12 within Visible Learning classrooms and see how visible learners grow and progress across time and content areas. Although you may identify with one of the teachers from a content perspective, we encourage you to read all of the vignettes to get a full sense of the variety of choices you can make in your instruction, based on your instructional goals.

In Chapter 1, we focus on the aspects of mathematics instruction that must be included in each lesson. We explore the components of effective mathematics instruction (conceptual, procedural, and application) and note that there is a need to recognize that student learning has to occur at the surface, deep, and transfer levels within each of these components. Surface, deep, and transfer learning served as the organizing feature of *Visible Learning for Mathematics*, and we will briefly review them and their value in learning. This book focuses on the ways in which teachers can develop students' surface, deep, and transfer learning, specifically by supporting students' conceptual understanding, procedural knowledge, and application whether with linear equations or integer operations. Finally, Chapter 1 contains information about the use of checks for understanding to monitor student learning. Generating evidence of learning is important for both teachers and students in determining the impact of the learning experiences and challenging mathematical tasks on learning. If learning is not happening, then we must make adjustments.

Following this introductory chapter, we turn our attention, separately, to each component of mathematics teaching and learning. However, we will walk through the process starting with the application of concepts and thinking skills, then direct our attention to conceptual understanding, and finally, procedural knowledge. This seemingly unconventional approach will allow us to start by making the goal or endgame visible: learners applying mathematics concepts and thinking skills to other situations or contexts.

Chapter 2 focuses on *application* of concepts and thinking skills. Returning to our three profiled classrooms, we will look at how we plan, develop, and implement challenging mathematical tasks that scaffold students' thinking as they apply their learning to new contexts or situations. Teaching mathematics in the Visible Learning classroom means supporting learners as they use mathematics in a variety of situations. In order for learners to effectively apply mathematical concepts and thinking skills to different situations, they must have strong conceptual understanding and procedural knowledge. Returning to Figure I.5, we will walk through the process for establishing clear learning intentions, defining evidence of learning, and developing challenging tasks that, as you already have come to expect, encourage learners to see themselves as their own teachers. Each chapter will discuss how to differentiate mathematical tasks by adjusting their difficulty and/or complexity, working to meet the needs of all learners in the mathematics classroom.

Chapters 3 and 4 take a similar approach with conceptual understanding and procedural knowledge, respectively. Using Chapter 2 as a reference point, we will return to the three profiled classrooms and explore the conceptual understanding and procedural knowledge that provided the foundation for their learners applying ideas to different mathematical situations. For example, what influences, strategies, actions, and approaches support a learner's conceptual understanding of systems of equations, measurement of circles, or integer operations? With conceptual understanding, what works best as we encourage learners to see mathematics as more than a set of mnemonics and procedures? Supporting students' thinking as they focus on underlying conceptual principles and properties, rather than relying on memory cues like PEMDAS, also necessitates adjusting the difficulty and complexity of mathematics tasks. As in Chapter 2, we will talk about differentiating tasks by adjusting their difficulty and complexity.

In this book, we do not want to discourage the value of procedural knowledge. Although mathematics is more than procedural knowledge, developing skills in basic procedures is needed for later work in each area of mathematics from the area and circumference of a circle to linear equations. As in the previous two chapters, Chapter 4 will look at what works best when in supporting students' fluency in procedural knowledge. Adjusting the difficulty and complexity of tasks will once again help us meet the needs of all learners.

In the final chapter of this book, we focus on how to make mathematics learning visible through evaluation. Teachers must have clear knowledge of their impact so that they can adjust the learning environment. Learners must have clear knowledge about their own learning so that they can be active in the learning process, plan the next steps, and understand what is behind the assessment. What does evaluation look like so that teachers can use it to plan instruction and to determine the impact that they have on learning? As part of Chapter 5, we highlight the value of feedback and explore the ways in which teachers can provide effective feedback to students that is growth producing. Furthermore, we will highlight how learners can engage in self-regulation feedback and provide feedback to their peers.

This book contains information on critical aspects of middle school mathematics instruction that have evidence for their ability to influence student learning. We're not suggesting that these be implemented in isolation but rather that they be combined into a series of linked learning experiences that result in students engaging in mathematics learning more fully and deliberately than they did before. Whether calculating slope or the area of a circle, we strive to create a mathematics classroom where we *see* learning through the eyes of our students and students *see* themselves as their own mathematics teachers. As learners progress from simplifying rational expressions to using ratios and proportions, teaching mathematics in the Visible Learning classroom should build and support assessment-capable visible mathematics learners.

TEACHING WITH CLARITY IN MATHEMATICS

1

CHAPTER 1 SUCCESS CRITERIA:

(1) I can describe teacher clarity and the process for providing clarity in my classroom.

(2) I can describe the components of effective mathematics instruction.

(3) I can relate the learning process to my own teaching and learning.

(4) I can give examples of how to differentiate mathematics tasks.

(5) I can describe the four different approaches to teaching mathematics.

In Ms. Ashley Norris's seventh grade mathematics class, students are learning to determine the percent increase or decrease in a given situation. On the board, she has clearly provided her learners with a **learning intention** and **success criteria** as follows:

Learning Intention: I am learning that percent increases and decreases are percents of change.

Success Criteria:

1. I can compute the percent increase or decrease.

2. I can determine which type of situation indicates an increase versus a decrease.

3. I can compare and contrast percent increases and percent decreases.

There are many different approaches for engaging learners in solving percent increase and decrease problems. Today, Ms. Norris provides her learners with a contextual situation and then, after assigning them to cooperative learning teams, asks learners to solve the following scenario:

You are helping your family shop for a new computer. You find a good laptop in the clearance section with two tags. It was marked down 15% and then all clearance items are 20% off their lowest price. The original cost of the laptop was $750. How much will you save on this purchase? How much can you spend on gaming headphones now and not exceed the $750 budget placed on you by your family?

Ms. Norris provides each cooperative learning team with different resources that they can choose to use in accomplishing this task. Groups that need additional scaffolding receive a worked example, while every group is offered a calculator or laptop with a spreadsheet application. She tells students that they can choose to use some, all, or none of the resources. As always, learners are encouraged to reference their textbooks and interactive mathematics notebooks as additional resources. Ms. Norris encourages her students to use any strategy that they believe would be appropriate for completing this task. One cooperative learning team did not find any of the resources helpful and decided to start calculating the answer by hand. Another cooperative learning team used the laptop computers to set up tables in a spreadsheet. One specific student asked, "Can we use our books and compare examples in the textbook with this problem?" Her team of learners did not find the resources helpful and began to discuss the information they found in the textbook. A fourth team of learners struggled with where to begin in answering the questions in this scenario. They did not immediately find any of the resources helpful and began to discuss the information they needed to "get started." Ms. Norris decides to provide these learners with a worked example to prompt their thinking about this particular problem. She is pleased that her learners are actively monitoring which strategy works best for them on this particular task.

Ms. Norris is implementing the principles of Visible Learning in her seventh grade mathematics classroom. Our intention is to help you implement these principles in your own classroom. By providing her learners with a challenging task, a clear learning intention, and success criteria, Ms. Norris's cooperative learning teams are developing conceptual understanding, gaining procedural knowledge, and applying their learning. She holds high expectations for her students in terms of both the difficulty and complexity of the task, as well as her learners' ability to deepen their mathematics learning by making learning visible to herself and each individual learner. As Ms. Norris monitors the learning progress in each team, holding all students accountable for their own learning, she takes opportunities to provide additional instruction when needed. Although her learners are engaged in cooperative learning with their peers, she regularly assesses her students for formative purposes. Ms. Norris is mobilizing principles of Visible Learning through her conscious awareness of her impact on student learning and her students are consciously aware of their learning through this challenging task. Ms. Norris works to accomplish this through these specific, intentional, and purposeful decisions in her mathematics instruction. She had clarity in her teaching of mathematics, allowing her learners to have clarity and see themselves as their own teachers (i.e., assessment-capable visible mathematics learners). This came about from using the following guiding questions in her planning and preparation for learning:

1. What do I want my students to learn?

2. What evidence shows that the learners have mastered the learning or are moving toward mastery?

Teaching Takeaway

As part of learning content, students should have access to and learn to apply a variety of strategies for solving problems.

EFFECT SIZE FOR STRATEGY MONITORING = 0.58

EFFECT SIZE FOR TEACHER CLARITY = 0.75

Video 3
What Does Teacher Clarity Mean in Middle School Mathematics?

https://resources.corwin.com/ vlmathematics-6-8

HOW VISIBLE TEACHING AND VISIBLE LEARNING COMPARE

Visible Teaching	Visible Learning
Clearly communicates the learning intention	So that learners understand the intention of the learning experience.
Identifies challenging success criteria	So that learners know what success looks like.
Utilizes a range of learning strategies	So that learners develop a range of learning strategies.
Continually monitors student learning	So that learners know when they are not progressing and can make adjustments.
Provides feedback to learners	So that learners can seek feedback about their learning.

Figure 1.1

online resources — This figure is available for download at resources.corwin.com/vlmathematics-6-8.

3. How will I check learners' understanding and progress?

4. What tasks will get my students to mastery?

5. How will I differentiate tasks to meet the needs of all learners?

6. What resources do I need?

7. How will I manage the learning?

> **Clarity** in learning means that both the teacher and the student know what the learning is for the day, why they are learning it, and what success looks like.

Ms. Norris exemplifies the relationship between Visible Teaching and Visible Learning (see Figure 1.1).

Now, let's look at how to achieve **clarity** in teaching mathematics by first understanding how components of mathematics learning interface with the learning progressions of the students in our classrooms. Then we will use this understanding to establish learning intentions, identify success criteria, create challenging mathematical tasks, and monitor or check for understanding.

Components of Effective Mathematics Learning

Mathematics is more than just memorizing formulas and then working problems with those formulas. Rather than a compilation of procedures—substituting a value for a variable in an expression, graphing a linear equation, plugging numbers into a simple interest formula, or dividing fractions—mathematics learning involves an interplay of conceptual understanding, procedural knowledge, and the application of mathematical concepts and thinking skills. Together these compose rigorous mathematics learning, which is furthered by the Standards for Mathematical Practice that claim students should

1. Make sense of problems and persevere in solving them.

2. Reason abstractly and quantitatively.

3. Construct viable arguments and critique the reasoning of others.

4. Model with mathematics.

5. Use appropriate tools strategically.

6. Attend to precision.

7. Look for and make use of structure.

8. Look for and express regularity in repeated reasoning (© Copyright 2010. National Governors Association Center for Best Practices and Council of Chief State School Officers. All rights reserved.).

Teaching mathematics in the Visible Learning classroom fosters student growth through attending to these mathematical practices or processes. As highlighted by Ms. Norris in the opening of this chapter, this comes from linked learning experiences and challenging mathematics tasks that make learning visible to both students and teachers.

Surface, Deep, and Transfer Learning

Each school year, regardless of the grade level, students develop their mathematics prowess through a progression that moves from understanding the surface contours of a concept into how to work with that concept efficiently by leveraging procedural skills as well as applying

THE RELATIONSHIP BETWEEN SURFACE, DEEP, AND TRANSFER LEARNING IN MATHEMATICS

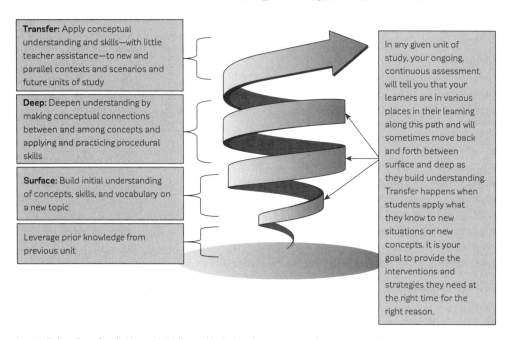

Transfer: Apply conceptual understanding and skills—with little teacher assistance—to new and parallel contexts and scenarios and future units of study

Deep: Deepen understanding by making conceptual connections between and among concepts and applying and practicing procedural skills

Surface: Build initial understanding of concepts, skills, and vocabulary on a new topic

Leverage prior knowledge from previous unit

In any given unit of study, your ongoing, continuous assessment will tell you that your learners are in various places in their learning along this path and will sometimes move back and forth between surface and deep as they build understanding. Transfer happens when students apply what they know to new situations or new concepts. It is your goal to provide the interventions and strategies they need at the right time for the right reason.

Source: Hattie, Fisher, Frey, Gojak, Moore, & Mellman (2017). Spiral Image copyright EssentialsCollection/iStock.com

Figure 1.2

Surface learning is the phase in which students build initial conceptual understanding of a mathematical idea and learn related vocabulary, representations, and procedural skills.

concepts and thinking skills to an ever-deepening exploration of what lies beneath mathematical ideas. For example, sixth graders transition from an emphasis on whole number operations to foundations for algebra. As another example, eighth graders transition from focusing on rational numbers to learning about other subsets of the real number system. Understanding these progressions requires that teachers consider the levels of learning expected from students. We think of three levels, or phases, of learning: surface, deep, and transfer (see Figure 1.2).

Learning is a process, not an event. With some conceptual understanding, procedural knowledge, and application, students may still only understand at the surface level. We do not define surface-level learning as superficial learning. Rather, we define **surface learning** as the initial development of conceptual understanding and procedural skill, with some application. In other words, this is the learners' initial learning around what a ratio is, the various representations of ratios and proportional relationships, and fundamental ideas about how to use ratios and proportions to solve problems. Surface learning is often misrepresented as rote rehearsal or memorization and is therefore not valued, but it is an essential part of the mathematics learning process. Students must understand how to represent ratios with manipulatives, in words or sketches, in real-world applications, and in equations to be able to connect these representations and use them in an authentic situation.

With the purposeful and intentional use of learning strategies that focus on how to relate and extend ideas, surface mathematics learning becomes deep learning. **Deep learning** occurs when students begin to make *connections* among conceptual ideas and procedural knowledge and apply their thinking with greater fluency. As learners begin to monitor their progress, adjust their learning, and select strategies to guide their learning, they more efficiently and effectively plan, investigate, elaborate on their knowledge, and make generalizations based on their experiences with mathematics content and processes.

If learners are to deepen their knowledge, they must regularly encounter situations that foster the transfer and generalization of their learning. The American Psychological Association (2015) notes that "student transfer or generalization of their knowledge and skills is not spontaneous or automatic" (p. 10) and **transfer learning** requires intentionally created events on the part of the teacher.

Figure 1.3 contains a representative list of strategies or influences organized by phase of learning. This is an updated list from *Visible Learning for Mathematics* (Hattie et al., 2017). Notice how many of these strategies and influences—clarity of learning goals, questioning, discourse, problem solving—align with the Effective Teaching Practices outlined by the National Council for Teachers of Mathematics (2014) in *Principles to Actions: Ensuring Mathematical Success for All* (see Figure 1.4).

For the influences from the Visible Learning research, we placed them in a specific phase based on the evidence of their impact and the outcomes that researchers use to document the impact each has on students' learning. For example, we have included concept maps and graphic organizers under deep learning. Learners will find it hard to organize

EFFECT SIZE FOR PRIOR ABILITY = 0.94 AND PRIOR ACHIEVEMENT = 0.55

Deep learning is a period when students consolidate their understanding and apply and extend some surface learning knowledge to support deeper conceptual understanding.

EFFECT SIZE FOR ELABORATION AND ORGANIZATION = 0.75

Transfer learning is the point at which students take their consolidated knowledge and skills and apply what they know to new scenarios and different contexts. It is also a time when students are able to think more metacognitively, reflecting on their own learning and understanding.

Surface Learning		Deep Learning		Transfer Learning	
Strategy	ES	Strategy	ES	Strategy	ES
Imagery	0.45	Inquiry-based teaching	0.40	Extended writing	0.44
Note taking	0.50	Questioning	0.48	Peer tutoring	0.53
Process skill: record keeping	0.52	Self-questioning	0.55	Synthesizing information across texts	0.63
Direct/deliberate instruction	0.60	Metacognitive strategy instruction	0.60	Problem-solving teaching	0.68
Organizing	0.60	Concept mapping	0.64	Formal discussions (e.g., debates)	0.82
Vocabulary programs	0.62	Reciprocal teaching	0.74	Organizing conceptual knowledge	0.85
Leveraging prior knowledge	0.65	Class discussion: discourse	0.82	Transforming conceptual knowledge	0.85
Mnemonics	0.76	Outlining and transforming notes	0.85	Identifying similarities and differences	1.32
Summarization	0.79	Small-group learning 0.47			
Integrating prior knowledge	0.93	Cooperative learning 0.40			
Teacher expectations 0.43					
Feedback 0.70					
Teacher clarity 0.75					
Integrated curricula programs 0.47					
Assessment-capable visible learner 1.33					

Source: Adapted from Almarode, Fisher, Frey, & Hattie (2018)

Figure 1.3

EFFECT SIZE FOR
METACOGNITIVE
STRATEGIES = 0.60
AND EVALUATION
AND REFLECTION
= 0.75

mathematics information or ideas if they do not yet understand that information whether it is a procedure, concept, or application. Without a conceptual understanding of volume and surface area, middle school mathematics students may approach these problems based on surface-level features (e.g., cylinders and cones both have a circular base, while pyramids and prisms both have polygonal bases) instead of deep-level

Establish mathematics goals to focus learning. Effective teaching of mathematics establishes clear goals for the mathematics that students are learning, situates goals within learning progressions, and uses the goals to guide instructional decisions.

Implement tasks that promote reasoning and problem solving. Effective teaching of mathematics engages students in solving and discussing tasks that promote mathematical reasoning and problem solving and allow multiple entry points and varied solution strategies.

Use and connect mathematical representations. Effective teaching of mathematics engages students in making connections among mathematical representations to deepen understanding of mathematics concepts and procedures and as tools for problem solving.

Facilitate meaningful mathematical discourse. Effective teaching of mathematics facilitates discourse among students to build shared understanding of mathematical ideas by analyzing and comparing student approaches and arguments.

Pose purposeful questions. Effective teaching of mathematics uses purposeful questions to assess and advance students' reasoning and sense making about important mathematical ideas and relationships.

Build procedural fluency from conceptual understanding. Effective teaching of mathematics builds fluency with procedures on a foundation of conceptual understanding so that students, over time, become skillful in using procedures flexibly as they solve contextual and mathematical problems.

Support productive struggle in learning mathematics. Effective teaching of mathematics consistently provides students, individually and collectively, with opportunities and supports to engage in productive struggle as they grapple with mathematical ideas and relationships.

Elicit and use evidence of student thinking. Effective teaching of mathematics uses evidence of student thinking to assess progress toward mathematical understanding and to adjust instruction continually in ways that support and extend learning.

Source: NCTM Teaching Practice Statements from National Council of Teachers of Mathematics (NCTM) (2014). *Principles to actions: Ensuring mathematical success for all.* Reston, VA: Author. Reprinted with permission.

Figure 1.4

features (e.g., seeing cylinders and prisms as similar to each other and different from cones or pyramids). When students have sufficient surface learning about specific content and processes, they are able to see the connections between multiple ideas and connect their specific knowledge of volume and surface area for particular figures with their spatial ability to decompose solid figures into known parts, which allow for the generalization of mathematics principles. As a reminder, two key findings from the Visible Learning research are as follows:

1. There is no one way to teach mathematics or one best instructional strategy that works in all situations for all students; and

2. We should not hold any influence, instructional strategy, action, or approach in higher esteem than students' learning.

As teachers, our conversations should focus on identifying where students are in their learning journey and moving them forward in their learning. This is best accomplished by talking about learning and measuring the impact that various approaches have on students' learning. If a given approach is not working, change it. If you experienced success with a particular strategy or approach in the past, give it a try but be ready to change if it does not work with this group of learners. Just because we can use FOIL or PEMDAS to find correct solutions, for example, does not mean those mnemonics will work for all students in your mathematics classroom—particularly if they lack understanding of the conceptual underpinnings of those procedures. Teachers have to monitor the impact that learning strategies have on students' mathematics learning and how they are progressing from surface to deep to transfer.

Moving Learners Through the Phases of Learning

The **SOLO Taxonomy** (Structure of Observed Learning Outcomes) (Biggs & Collis, 1982) conceptualizes the movement from surface to deep to transfer learning as a process of first branching out and then strengthening connections between ideas (Figure 1.5).

As you reflect on your own students, you can likely think of learners that have limited to no prior experiences with certain mathematics content. Take, for example, ratios and proportional reasoning. Although learners have likely encountered real-world uses of these concepts (e.g., speed in miles per hour and scale models), many have had no experience with the mathematics behind those real-world applications. Thus, they have no relevant structure to their thinking. This means they likely struggle to articulate a single idea about the specific content. Another example of this occurs with equations or formulas. Students recognize that letters

THE SOLO TAXONOMY

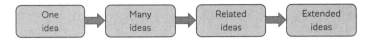

Source: Adapted from Biggs & Collis, 1982.

Figure 1.5

represent specific items in an equation, say $A = \frac{1}{2}(b \times h)$, but they are not able to identify these features in a triangle or make inferences about the effect on area if the base of a triangle is held constant and the height increased by a factor of 2. This part of the SOLO Taxonomy is referred to as the prestructural level or prestructural thinking. At the prestructural level, learners may focus on irrelevant ideas, avoid engaging in the content, or not know where to start. This requires the teacher to support the learner in acquiring and building background knowledge. When teachers clearly recognize that learners are at the prestructural level, the learning experience should aim to build surface learning around concepts, procedures, and applications.

Surface Learning in the Middle School Mathematics Classroom

As learners progress in their thinking, they may develop single ideas or a single aspect related to a concept. Learners at this level can identify and name shapes or attributes, follow simple procedures, highlight single aspects of a concept, and solve one type of problem (Hook & Mills, 2011). They know that $A = \frac{1}{2}(b \times h)$ calculates the area of a triangle, b represents the base, and h represents the height. They can only solve problems involving the exact type of triangle provided in an in-class example, such as in Figure 1.6.

For example, some learners can calculate the area of a right triangle only. Any variation to the problem will pose a significant challenge to these learners, requiring additional instruction (e.g., finding the area of a right triangle versus an isosceles or scalene triangle). With the right strategy at

Teaching Takeaway

In the surface phase of learning, a student may be able to identify and name shapes or attributes, follow simple procedures, highlight single aspects of a concept, or solve one type of problem.

27

EXAMPLES OF DIFFERENT PROBLEMS INVOLVING A TRIANGLE

What is the area of the triangle?

☐ units²

There are 2 things you'll need to be able to do with non-right-angle triangles:

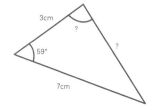

1. How would I find the **missing side and angle**?
2. How do I find the **area** of this non-right-angle triangle?

What is the area of the triangle?

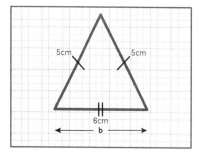

What is the area of the triangle?

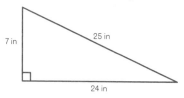

Figure 1.6

the right time, learners will continue to build surface learning by acquiring multiple ideas about concepts, procedures, and applications. Learners can then solve problems involving different types of triangles (e.g., right triangles, isosceles triangles, and equilateral triangles) and describe coherently how to calculate the area of any triangle instead of simply executing the algorithm. However, each variation of a triangle is seen as a distinct scenario, not connected to the other variations of triangles.

Like Ms. Norris, all teachers should establish learning intentions and success criteria based on where students are in their learning progression. Moving away from triangles and back to Ms. Norris's classroom, let us look at how we can develop learning intentions and success criteria for conceptual understanding, procedural knowledge, and application for learners at these two levels (one idea and many ideas) (Figures 1.7 and 1.8).

SURFACE-PHASE LEARNING INTENTIONS FOR EACH COMPONENT OF MATHEMATICS LEARNING

Learning Intentions	Conceptual Understanding	Procedural Knowledge	Application of Concepts and Thinking Skills
Unistructural (one idea)	I am learning that a percent is a special ratio.	I am learning that a percent can be represented as a ratio.	I am learning that percentages and some ratios represent a part to whole relationship.
Multistructural (many ideas)	I am learning the relationship between proportions, percents, and ratios.	I am learning that percentages allow me to solve problems involving change.	I am learning that ratios and percents can be used to represent change.

Figure 1.7

SURFACE-PHASE SUCCESS CRITERIA FOR EACH COMPONENT OF MATHEMATICS LEARNING

Success Criteria	Conceptual Understanding	Procedural Knowledge	Application of Concepts and Thinking Skills
Unistructural (one idea)	I can describe how a percent can be represented as a ratio.	I can write a ratio given a percent.	I can explain sales tax, discounts, or mark-up using percents.
Multistructural (many ideas)	I can explain how percent change can be represented as a proportion.	I can calculate percent change.	I can use an equation to calculate the amount of change (e.g., interest, sales tax, etc.).

Figure 1.8

Deep Learning in the Middle School Mathematics Classroom

Biggs and Collis (1982) conceptualize deep learning as identifying relationships between concepts or ideas. Learners at the deep level of the learning process focus on relationships and relational thinking about concepts, procedures, and applications. Returning to the area of a

Teaching Takeaway

Learners in the deep phase can identify relationships between concepts and draw connections between concepts, procedures, and applications.

triangle, learners are able to compare and contrast the procedure for finding the area of right, acute, and obtuse triangles. Conceptually, learners deepen their understanding of base, height, and the relationship of these two values to the area of the triangle. They can analyze a specific situation and determine the best approach to finding the area of the triangle without specific guidance on which approach is most efficient and effective. The development of relational thinking paves the way for transferring these concepts and thinking, or as Biggs and Collis (1982) call it, extending thinking.

The learning intentions and success criteria should reflect this level of thinking or readiness for our learners (Figures 1.9 and 1.10).

DEEP-PHASE LEARNING INTENTIONS FOR EACH COMPONENT OF MATHEMATICS LEARNING

Learning Intentions	Conceptual Understanding	Procedural Knowledge	Application of Concepts and Thinking Skills
Relational (related ideas)	I am learning that the specific context of the situation determines how to best represent the relationship (e.g., increase, decrease, mark-up, discount, interest, etc.).	I am learning that calculating the percent increase or decrease depends on the specific situation.	I am learning to represent constraints using proportions, ratios, and percents.

Figure 1.9

DEEP-PHASE SUCCESS CRITERIA FOR EACH COMPONENT OF MATHEMATICS LEARNING

Success Criteria	Conceptual Understanding	Procedural Knowledge	Application of Concepts and Thinking Skills
Relational (related ideas)	I can explain the relationship(s) between terms in equations involving percentages, ratios, and proportions.	I can create equations to solve problems involving ratios, percents, and proportions.	I can use equations to solve problems involving interest.

Figure 1.10

Transfer Learning in the Middle School Mathematics Classroom

The next step in the SOLO progression is for the learner to transfer learning to different contexts. At the extended level of thinking, learners formulate big ideas and generalize their learning to a new domain. For example, an extended abstract thinker might predict how the area of a triangle varies as the height is increased or decreased, leaving the base constant. Learners at this level may begin to generalize this to other two-dimensional geometric shapes, recognizing that there are dimensions that maximize the area of a specific shape. Learners will begin to

TRANSFER-PHASE LEARNING INTENTIONS FOR EACH COMPONENT OF MATHEMATICS LEARNING

Learning Intentions	Conceptual Understanding	Procedural Knowledge	Application of Concepts and Thinking Skills
Extended abstract (extending ideas)	I am learning that equations represent numeric relationships in authentic situations.	I am learning that equations can be rearranged to highlight quantities of focus.	I am learning to use equations to make inferences (e.g., investments).

Figure 1.11

TRANSFER-PHASE SUCCESS CRITERIA FOR EACH COMPONENT OF MATHEMATICS LEARNING

Success Criteria	Conceptual Understanding	Procedural Knowledge	Application of Concepts and Thinking Skills
Extended abstract (extending ideas)	I can interpret solutions to problems involving percentages as viable or nonviable solutions in the specific context.	I can rearrange equations to focus on a quantity of interest.	I can compute the simple interest and new balance earned in an investment given number of years.

Figure 1.12

extend their thinking by using procedures in very different situations. For example, they might connect the height of a triangle to the height of a parallelogram, realizing that the term plays a similar role in the area calculations for each shape.

Being clear about the learning intentions and success criteria is just as important in extending student ideas as with the previous levels of thinking (Figures 1.11 and 1.12).

With clear learning intentions and success criteria in place, we must design learning experiences and challenging mathematics tasks that result in students engaging in both mathematical content and processes at the right level of thinking. This brings us to the question of rigor.

Differentiating Tasks for Complexity and Difficulty

As we have noted, there are three phases to student learning: surface, deep, and transfer. Teachers have to plan tasks that provide students opportunities to learn and progress through these stages, as well as the flexibility to return to different phases of the learning when necessary. When students experience a "Goldilocks" challenge, the effect size is 0.74. A Goldilocks challenge is not too hard and not too boring. For example, if learners need additional surface learning around some aspect of procedural knowledge or conceptual understanding, we have the flexibility to go back, provide that instructional support, and then continue in the learning. The type of task matters as students move along in their thinking from surface to deep to transfer. In *Visible Learning for Mathematics*, we shared the Common Core State Standards for Mathematics definition of rigor as the balance of conceptual learning, procedural skills and fluency, and application. This is a good definition when applied to mathematics instruction, curricula, and learning as a whole. But we also want to address the appropriate challenge of any individual mathematical *task*. In this book, we are using the term **rigor** to mean the balance of complexity and difficulty of a mathematical task.

As soon as someone mentions "rigorous tasks," we mentally formulate what those are in our own classrooms. Is rigor completing 50 problems for homework? Is rigor engaging in a mathematics brainteaser? To effectively design rigorous mathematics tasks that align with our learning intentions and success criteria, we have to better understand what is meant by difficulty and complexity. *Difficulty* is the amount of effort or work expected of the student, whereas *complexity* is the level of thinking, the number of steps, or the abstractness of the task. We can differentiate by adjusting the level of difficulty and/or complexity for any task regardless of whether the task focuses on conceptual understanding, procedural knowledge, or the application. In middle school, learners are expected to recognize and represent proportional relationships between quantities. The success criteria at one point in the middle school mathematics learning progression might be as follows:

1. I can determine if two quantities are in a proportional relationship.

2. I can identify the constant of proportionality.

For the above success criteria, the teacher could lower the difficulty of tasks, while maintaining the level of complexity set by the success criteria, by allowing learners to analyze the relationship using ratio tables or graphs constructed with structured digital tools, filling in values, and observing the results. Similarly, learners could identify the constant of proportionality in relationships where the numbers are friendlier. As learners develop greater procedural fluency and conceptual understanding, the level of difficulty could be increased by requiring the learner to identify the constant of proportionality from a graph where the value at $(1, r)$ is not straightforward to compute.

We do not believe that teachers can radically impact student learning by making them do a lot more work. Practicing hundreds of fraction division problems (increased difficulty) will not extend their thinking. Similarly, asking students to engage in a task that is far too complex or not complex enough for their current level of thinking can also reduce the impact on student learning. Instead, we should balance difficulty and complexity in the design of learning tasks. Throughout this book, we will return to the concepts of difficulty and complexity as we discuss the various strategies and tasks our three profiled teachers use and share how they can adjust the difficulty and complexity of those tasks to meet the needs of all learners.

Teaching Takeaway

We can differentiate mathematics tasks by adjusting the difficulty and complexity of the task.

EFFECT SIZE FOR SPACED VERSUS MASS PRACTICE = 0.60

EFFECT SIZE FOR "RIGHT" LEVEL OF CHALLENGE = 0.74

Teaching Takeaway

Learning tasks should balance conceptual understanding, procedural knowledge, and application in our mathematics classrooms. We should differentiate those tasks by adjusting the difficulty and complexity.

EFFECT SIZE
FOR DIRECT/
DELIBERATE
INSTRUCTION
= 0.60

Guided practice involves the teacher and the students collaboratively engaged in problem solving. This helps the teacher and learners determine when students are ready to work independently.

EFFECT SIZE FOR
SCAFFOLDING
= 0.82

EFFECT SIZE
FOR DELIBERATE
PRACTICE = 0.79

EFFECT SIZE FOR
FEEDBACK = 0.70

Just as task design is an important consideration in the Visible Learning classroom, learners need to experience a *wide range* of tasks if they are going to become assessment-capable visible learners. They need opportunities to work with their teacher, with their peers, and independently so that they develop the social and academic skills necessary to continue to learn on their own. Although Ms. Norris decided to use a peer-led dialogic approach, this is just one of four approaches to mathematics instruction. Three additional approaches are deliberate instruction, teacher- or student-led dialogic instruction, and independent learning.

Deliberate Instruction. Deliberate instruction, commonly referred to as direct instruction, has a negative reputation in education. This approach is mistakenly assumed to be synonymous with lecture. That is not the case. Deliberate instruction involves

- Activation of prior knowledge
- Introduction of the new concept or skill
- Guided practice of the concept or skill
- Feedback on the guided practice
- Independent practice

To limit one's understanding of direct/deliberate instruction to highly scripted programs or lecture is to overlook the practices that make it highly effective for developing surface-level knowledge. With an effect size of 0.59, direct/deliberate instruction offers a pedagogical pathway that provides students with the modeling, scaffolding, and practice they require when learning new concepts and skills. "When we learn something new . . . we need more skill development and content; as we progress, we need more connections, relationships, and schemas to organize these skills and content; we then need more regulation or self-control over how we continue to learn the content and ideas" (Hattie, 2009, p. 84).

Teacher-Led Dialogic. As learners develop the skills to engage in deepening dialogue, teacher-led dialogue allows the teacher to be present in student discussions about mathematics, facilitating the process to scaffold student conversation. In the end, the teacher will fade his or her support as students develop the necessary skills to take over and lead the conversations on their own. Teacher-led dialogic instruction does not require deliberate instruction first. Instead, this approach requires learners to possess the surface knowledge necessary to engage in deeper dialogue. For example, a teacher may utilize a teacher-led dialogic approach as she introduces the reasoning necessary to recognize a proportional relationship in similar figures. Over time, after modeling the type of questioning and reasoning, the geometry teacher's role in this dialogue will lessen, gradually releasing the students to more independent work (i.e., less dependent on the teacher).

Student-Led Dialogic. Adolescents have a way of making themselves understood by their peers. In other words, students' thoughts and explanations can propel the learning of their peers. Whether solving problems, providing feedback, or engaging in reciprocal teaching, the collaborative act of peer-assisted learning in mathematics benefits all students in the exchange. In student-led dialogic learning, the role of the teacher is to organize and facilitate, but it is the students who are the ones that lead the discussion.

Independent. The learning continues, and in fact deepens, when students are able to employ what they have been learning. This can occur in three possible ways (Fisher & Frey, 2008):

- Fluency building
- Spiral review
- Extension

Fluency building is especially effective when students are in the surface learning phase and need spaced practice opportunities to strengthen automaticity. For instance, students who play online mathematics games, or engage in independent practice, are engaged in fluency-building independent learning.

A spiral review is one in which students revisit previously mastered content in order to prevent learning recidivism due to infrequent use. For instance, an entrance ticket, exit ticket, or homework assignment draws from content that was introduced in a previous week, unit, or quarter.

Teaching Takeaway

These approaches are in no particular order. Using the right approach at the right time increases our impact on student learning in the mathematics classroom.

EFFECT SIZE FOR QUESTIONING = 0.48

EFFECT SIZE FOR SELF-VERBALIZATION AND SELF-QUESTIONING = 0.55

EFFECT SIZE FOR HELP SEEKING = 0.83

EFFECT SIZE FOR SELF-REGULATION STRATEGIES = 0.52

There is no one way to teach mathematics. We should not hold any influence, instructional strategy, action, or approach to teaching and learning in higher esteem than students' learning.

Extension promotes transfer and occurs when learners are asked to use what they have learned in a new way. Independent learning through extension includes writing about mathematics, teaching information to peers, and engaging in mathematics investigations.

Checks for Understanding

Checks for understanding offer both teachers and learners the opportunity to monitor the learning process as students engage in challenging tasks and progress toward the learning intention. To ensure the learning is visible in our mathematics classroom, we must have the necessary information about student progress so that we provide effective feedback. In addition, learners must also have the necessary information about their progress so that they can effectively monitor progress and adjust their learning. Using the success criteria as a guide, checks for understanding include any strategies, activities, or tasks that make student thinking visible and allow both the teacher and learner to observe learning progress. When we are planning, developing, and implementing checks for understanding, two essential questions should guide our thinking:

Guiding Questions for Creating Opportunities to Respond

1. What checks for understanding will tell me and my learners how they are progressing in their learning related to the Learning Intention(s) and Success Criteria?

2. What are we going to do with this information that will help students with their next steps in learning this content?

EFFECT SIZE FOR PROVIDING FORMATIVE EVALUATION = 0.48

Checks for understanding give us feedback about the impact of our teaching and should be driven by the learning intention and success criteria for that particular lesson or learning experience. For example, if the success criteria say, *describe*, then the check for understanding should focus on or provide deliberate practice in *describing*. Someone teaching mathematics in the Visible Learning classroom should focus on assessment for the purpose of informing instructional decisions and providing feedback to learners. The following assumptions inform our collective understanding about teaching and learning:

1. Assessment occurs throughout the academic year, and the results are used to inform the teacher and the learner. Each period, time is set aside to understand students' mathematics learning progress and provide feedback to learners.

2. A meaningful amount of time is dedicated to developing mathematics content and processes. Across every unit, students engage in sustained, organized, and comprehensive experiences with all of the components: conceptual understanding, procedural knowledge, and application of concepts and thinking skills.

3. Solving problems and discussing tasks occurs every class period. These events occur with the teacher, with peers, and independently.

Profiles of Three Teachers

In addition to the videos accompanying each chapter of this book, we will follow the practices of three teachers throughout the remaining chapters. Just as we have provided specific examples throughout this chapter and in the videos, we will devote more time to take an in-depth look into the classrooms of three middle school mathematics teachers. We will give you a front-row seat as they make specific, intentional, and purposeful decisions in teaching mathematics in the Visible Learning classroom.

Joanna Halstrom

Joanna Halstrom is a seventh grade mathematics teacher in Michigan. She has taught every grade in middle school, but this year has only seventh graders. Her experience across all three grade levels has allowed her to work with a team of teachers who started with their learners in sixth grade and will be looping up with them through eighth grade. Ms. Halstrom's multi-grade level experience gives her a vertical perspective on mathematics knowledge, procedures, and concepts as well as the learning progressions of her students. As Ms. Halstrom says, "I've known almost all of my students since they were in sixth grade, so I know their interests and strengths. We got the year off to a great start because I knew exactly what I needed to be working on in mathematics." Ms. Halstrom teaches five periods per day, with an average of 36 learners

> **Teaching Takeaway**
>
> Unless we, as teachers, have clear success criteria, we are hardly likely to develop good checks for understanding for our learners.

in each of her classes. Her school is ethnically diverse, and two-thirds of the students are Arab-American. Over 75% of her learners speak a language in addition to English. Her school qualifies as a school-wide Title I school, with 42% of the students qualifying for free lunch (a measure of poverty). In addition, 10% of the students receive special education services. Ms. Halstrom is working to incorporate new instructional materials into her teaching and her students' learning that her district just purchased last year. As she notes, "There is so much to offer in these materials, but I sometimes get lost in them. I am lucky to have a great team that collaborates with each other so that we can figure out how to use the materials for the greatest impact."

Luciana Fernandez

Luciana Fernandez teaches eighth grade mathematics and algebra in California. At her school, eighth grade students do not need to pass any type of preassessment or screening test to enroll in different levels of mathematics courses (i.e., eighth grade mathematics versus Algebra 1). In California, there are requirements that schools and districts articulate their math course pathway and the requirements for entrance into each class. For Ms. Fernandez, algebraic thinking is the default curriculum and she believes that all students can master this type of thinking. She works very hard to emphasize algebraic thinking each and every day, pushing back against a focus only on procedures (e.g., the concept of a solution to an equation versus the steps to solving an equation). Ms. Fernandez teaches three periods of eighth grade mathematics per day and two periods of algebra per day. Her classes are very short, at 48 minutes each. Her learners are mainly Latino (80%) and speak Spanish as their heritage language. All of the students in the school qualify for free lunch and 19% of the students receive special education services. As Ms. Fernandez says, "Mathematics is another language, and my students are skilled at learning language so I'm never surprised by their performance. They love the rich tasks we engage with and they see math as an important part of what they need to learn to have a good life."

Jasvinder Singh

Jasvinder Singh is a sixth grade mathematics teacher in Virginia. He is part of a four-person team that shares the same learners. His team includes a humanities teacher who teaches English and history, a science teacher who also teaches an elective rotation, and a special education teacher who provides accommodations, modifications, and small group instruction for the 98 students that they share. This is a large middle school in which each grade level has at least two teams. For example, there is a second four-person team in sixth grade as well as a two-person team that provides instruction to a smaller group of 33 to 35 learners. As part of his own learning journey, Mr. Singh earned a math specialist certificate and wanted to share his knowledge of mathematics with more students. The group of learners on Mr. Singh's team is diverse, with 80% of them qualifying for free or reduced school lunch. Sixty percent of the students are female, 45% are African American, 35% are Latino/Hispanic, 15% are Asian-Pacific Islander, 4% are Caucasian, and 1% are other races or ethnicities. Of the 98 students, 14 have disabilities and all of the learners have a wide range of instructional needs. Mr. Singh says, "We are the bridge between elementary school and their full class rotations in seventh grade when they will have six periods per day. Because of our schedule, I get about 85 minutes per day with each group of students, which is great to really help build their confidence and conceptual knowledge in mathematics."

These three teachers, although in different regions and contexts, operate under three important assumptions:

1. There is no one way to teach mathematics or one best instructional strategy that works in all situations for all students, but there is compelling evidence for tools that can help students reach their learning goals.

2. We should not hold any influence, instructional strategy, action, or approach to teaching and learning in higher esteem than students' learning.

3. Effective teaching and learning require establishing clear learning intentions and success criteria, designing learning experiences and challenging mathematics tasks, monitoring student progress, providing feedback, and adjusting lessons based on the learning of students.

In the chapters that follow, you will encounter these three teachers and view the lesson plans they have developed for themselves. In order to establish a predictable pattern for displaying this information, we will use the planning for clarity questions described in Figure I.5. Lessons based on these guiding questions are not meant to be delivered in a strictly linear fashion; rather, they are intended to serve as a way to guide your thinking about the elements of the lesson. In addition, through the videos accompanying this book, you will more briefly meet a number of teachers from other grade levels whose practices illustrate the approaches under discussion. Although no book on lesson planning could ever entirely capture every context or circumstance you encounter, we hope that the net effect is that we provide a process for representing methods for incorporating Visible Learning for mathematics consistently in your middle school classroom.

Reflection

Mathematics instruction that capitalizes on Visible Learning is established upon principles of learning. Recognizing that learners develop procedural knowledge, improve conceptual understanding, and apply concepts and thinking by engaging in surface, deep, and transfer learning allows us to intentionally and purposefully foster increasingly deeper and more sophisticated types of thinking in mathematics. This focus on the individual learner makes this approach inclusive of all learners, including those with language or additional learning needs. Teaching mathematics in the Visible Learning classroom means leveraging high-impact instruction to accelerate student learning through surface, deep, and transfer phases of learning by engaging them in strategies, actions, and approaches to learning at the right time and for the right content. These challenging learning tasks have clear learning intentions and success criteria that allow students to engage in a variety of ways and with a variety of materials. Learning becomes visible for the teacher and the students. In other words, an assessment-capable visible mathematics learner notices when he or she is learning and is proactive in making sure that learning is obvious. As we engage in discussions about mathematics learning in this book, we will return to these indicators that students are visible mathematics learners to explore how they might look in the classroom.

1. Take a moment and develop your own explanation of teacher clarity. What does teacher clarity look like in your mathematics classroom?

2. Using an upcoming lesson plan as an example, what components of mathematics instruction are you focusing on in the lesson? How does your lesson incorporate all or some of the following?

    a. Making sense of problems and persevering in solving them

    b. Reasoning abstractly and quantitatively

    c. Constructing viable arguments and critiquing the reasoning of others

    d. Modeling with mathematics

    e. Using appropriate tools strategically

    f. Attending to precision

    g. Looking for and making use of structure

    h. Looking for and expressing regularity in repeated reasoning

3. Using that same lesson plan, how will you or could you adjust the difficulty and/or complexity of the mathematics tasks to meet the needs of all learners?

4. Give some examples of learners engaged in surface learning, deep learning, and transfer learning. What are the observed learning outcomes of these students? What learning experiences best support learners at each level?

TEACHING FOR THE APPLICATION OF CONCEPTS AND THINKING SKILLS

2

CHAPTER 2 SUCCESS CRITERIA:

(1) I can describe what teaching for the application of concepts and thinking skills in the mathematics classroom looks like.

(2) I can apply the Teaching for Clarity Planning Guide to teaching for application.

(3) I can compare and contrast different approaches to teaching for application.

(4) I can give examples of how to differentiate the complexity and difficulty of mathematics tasks designed for application.

Assessment-capable visible learners in the middle school mathematics classroom use mathematics in situations that require mathematics concepts and thinking skills. How efficiently and effectively this occurs depends on the learners' conceptual understanding and procedural knowledge. This is where we begin our classroom journey, the application of concepts and thinking skills. When planning for clarity (see Figure I.5), we begin with the end in mind and we ask ourselves, "What do I want my students to learn?"

In this chapter, we take the same approach. Ms. Halstrom, Ms. Fernandez, and Mr. Singh focus on the end goal for each of their learners. All three teachers expect their learners to apply mathematics concepts and thinking skills to authentic situations. Thus, our journey begins with how these three teachers, by design, teach for this purpose. The QR codes in the margin provide video examples of application in action from a middle school mathematics classroom. In Chapters 3 and 4, we will go back in time and look at how these classrooms got here.

The nature of the application of concepts and thinking skills differs *across* the three classrooms and *within* the three classrooms. How each teacher approaches this depends on the learning needs of the students in his or her classroom. Therefore, you will see that Ms. Halstrom, Ms. Fernandez, and Mr. Singh adjust the rigor—or complexity and difficulty—of the application task, depending on where their learners currently are in the learning process (e.g., surface, deep, or transfer). For example, Ms. Fernandez adjusts the rigor of her application task for learners who need additional surface learning around the specific application task. Likewise, Ms. Halstrom and Mr. Singh adjust the rigor of their application task to support learners who have gaps in their conceptual understanding. In all three classrooms, there are learners who can not only apply concepts and thinking skills to authentic scenarios but also transfer them to very different contexts and scenarios. You will see this type of transfer as well. As we journey through these three classrooms, pay special attention to how each teacher differentiates the complexity and difficulty of the mathematics tasks so that all learners have access and the opportunity to apply concepts and thinking skills.

Ms. Halstrom and Circles and Cylinders

Today is the day Ms. Halstrom's learners apply their learning about three-dimensional objects and circles to authentic problem-solving scenarios. The unit has been full of hands-on experiences, and students have built both conceptual understanding and procedural fluency in calculating the area and circumference of a circle. Now, Ms. Halstrom wants students to apply what they have learned to three-dimensional objects. Students have previously studied properties of three-dimensional objects with polygonal faces, including the idea of surface area, and today they will connect this to their understanding of circles.

EFFECT SIZE FOR PRIOR ACHIEVEMENT = 0.55 AND PRIOR ABILITY = 0.94

Ms. Halstrom is pleased that the art teacher collaborated with her on a task that asks learners to design signs or labels that will be affixed to different cylindrical objects, which will be presented at the school's spring festival (Figure 2.1).

DIFFERENT CYLINDRICAL OBJECTS FOR WHICH MS. HALSTROM'S LEARNERS WILL DESIGN LABELS AND SIGNS

a. (water cooler)

Source: Danni1185/iStock .com

b. (utility pole)

Source: careyhaider/ iStock.com

c. (lamp post)

Source: terex/iStock .com

d. (water bottle)

Source: Shablon/ iStock.com

e. (outdoor garbage can)

Source: stacey_newman/ iStock.com

Figure 2.1

The rigor of today's mathematics task comes front and center as students use what they have learned to create signs or labels for cylindrical objects with various dimensions. In terms of complexity, learners must assimilate multiple attributes of each cylindrical object with their conceptual understanding and procedural knowledge of cylindrical objects. Irregular shapes provide a more complex context to which learners have to apply their thinking. With regard to difficulty, some of the cylindrical objects will require more effort due to specific attributes (i.e., size) rather than the complexity of multiple attributes.

Ms. Halstrom is confident from the work she has seen that her students know the formulas for area and circumference of circles. They can explain where the formulas come from and use them to compute area and circumference accurately. Many are using calculators for this particular unit, which is okay with her as long as they can confirm with an estimate that their answer is appropriate.

What Ms. Halstrom Wants Her Students to Learn

Ms. Halstrom is focusing on the following standards today:

MATHEMATICS CONTENT AND PRACTICE STANDARDS

7.G.B

Solve real-life and mathematical problems involving angle measure, area, surface area, and volume.

7.G.B.4

Know the formulas for the surface area and circumference of a circle and use them to solve problems.

Ms. Halstrom is helping her learners develop the following Standards for Mathematical Practice:

- Make sense of problems and persevere in solving them.
- Model with mathematics.

This lesson focuses on the "use them to solve problems" part of the above mathematics content standard. Students will stretch their thinking through this challenge and will need to make sense of the task and work to find a solution. As part of the problem-solving process, learners will create a model of a specific object to address their assigned problem.

Learning Intentions and Success Criteria

Although these standards guide the end goals of instruction, the wording is not particularly useful to the students in understanding what is expected of them in this specific lesson. To make today's learning visible to her students, Ms. Halstrom develops learning intentions and success criteria for this specific application task. Her approach is to develop learning intentions for content, language, and social dimensions of the experience. Dividing learning intentions into *content*, *language*, and *social* varieties can provide teachers and students alike a clearer sense of the day's expectations. **Content learning intentions** answer the question for students: "What is the math I am supposed to use and learn today?" **Language learning intentions** give teachers a space to lay out the language demands of the day: Are students developing new academic or content vocabulary, are they practicing recently developed vocabulary within proper linguistic structures, or are they utilizing those structures toward their actual communicative functions? Language learning intentions answer the question for students: "How should I communicate my mathematical thinking today?" This is not limited to verbal communication and can include written or visual representations of mathematical thinking. **Social learning intentions** allow teachers to develop and leverage social and sociomathematical norms within their classroom culture. Social learning intentions answer the question for students: "How should I interact with my learning community today?"

Ms. Halstrom's learning intentions for this lesson are as follows:

Content Learning Intention: I am learning to apply my understanding of area and circumference of circles to surface area of cylindrical objects when deciding how large a sign or label should be.

(Continued)

Video 4
Learning Intentions in an Application Lesson

https://resources.corwin.com/vlmathematics-6-8

Content learning intentions: What is the math I am supposed to use and learn today?

Language learning intentions: How should I communicate my mathematical thinking today?

Social learning intentions: How should I interact with my learning community today?

EFFECT SIZE FOR TEACHING COMMUNICATION SKILLS AND STRATEGIES = 0.43

(Continued)

Language Learning Intention: I am learning to use mathematics vocabulary (circumference, diameter, area, surface area, height) when solving problems related to cylindrical objects.

Social Learning Intention: I am learning to engage in productive discussions about how my peers approached their specific problem—including their reasoning and modeling of the scenario.

These learning intentions share more clearly what Ms. Halstrom is looking for in today's work. This content standard is the main focus of the entire unit of study, so her students need more specific guidance and expectations each day. These specific learning intentions also bring in connections to other standards reflected in this activity. Although students are familiar with the concept of surface area, they have not explicitly applied it to cylinders as they will today. This task will promote reasoning and problem solving for Ms. Halstrom's students as they make the connections between the concepts of surface area, circumference, and cylindrical objects.

While Ms. Halstrom endeavors to make connections to an authentic context and scenario frequently in her teaching, she is most deliberate about it in this type of learning experience. The more students can see their mathematics being used in their world, the more they understand its inherent and natural relevance.

As Ms. Halstrom decides how to communicate success criteria to her students so that they can self-assess their progress, she considers what success looks like in today's lesson. She will know her students are successful in this lesson if they are able to calculate their assigned sign and label dimensions correctly. The ultimate success criterion will be that the signs and labels fit accurately, but that will not be tested until the school festival itself. Therefore, learners will have to construct models of the cylindrical objects and use those models to develop their labels. Ms. Halstrom will also be listening and watching for students' use of appropriate vocabulary in their discussions and writing.

Ms. Halstrom knows that there are several challenges for students in this task. Students must figure out how circumference relates to the dimensions of their label or sign. They are responsible for determining the height of their label or sign—how much of the object's vertical distance should be covered. They are responsible for determining how to affix the signs to the objects from a menu of three choices. The success criteria for the day are as follows:

☐ I can calculate the surface area of a cylinder.

☐ I can explain how the dimensions of a cylindrical object relate to the surface area.

☐ I can describe the relationship between the circumference of a circle and surface area.

☐ I can determine appropriate dimensions for the label for each object based on the size of the object and attachment method selected.

To further support the success criteria for today, Ms. Halstrom has pictures ready to show the class what each method of attachment looks like so they can think about which is best in a given situation. This includes strategic decisions about how much of the bottle the students want their label to cover (e.g., the entire bottle or just the area below the slope of the bottle). Ms. Halstrom has sample water bottles and drink coolers for students to measure.

> EFFECT SIZE FOR IMAGERY = 0.45

Guiding and Scaffolding Student Thinking

As the class enters the room, Ms. Halstrom has some images from last year's event displayed on the screen. She launches the task by telling the class that they will be deciding the theme and creating the designs in art class, but they will use their time in today's math class to determine the size of various signs and labels so they can use that information to make good decisions about what signs or labels to create. She shows the class a list of the objects they will be considering:

- Large drink coolers
- Lamp posts
- Utility poles

- Water bottles
- Outdoor garbage cans

Sensing a theme, one student gets up and goes to the window. "The trash cans are round. Ms. Halstrom, all these things are round!"

Their teacher responds, "Precisely, because we are studying circles." Ms. Halstrom distributes a label size calculations chart for each pair of students to complete.

As part of her planning, Ms. Halstrom has assigned each pair of students two objects they must measure and calculate and then work on others as they wish. This allows her to better match the difficulty and complexity of the task to students' learning needs. For example, some learners will be assigned less complex objects (e.g., a cylindrical drink cooler versus a water bottle with a sloping neck), while others will be assigned objects with more difficult dimensions to measure (e.g., lamp post and utility pole).

Label Size Calculations

Use what you have learned about finding the circumference of a circle to help you calculate the right-size label or sign for each object below.

Your label size depends on two things: the size of the object and the way you attach the label.

Object	Diameter	Circumference	Height	Exact Dimensions	Attachment Style	Working Dimensions
Drink Cooler						
Lamp Post						
Utility Pole						
Water Bottle						
Garbage Can						

online resources ▶ This chart is available for download at resources.corwin.com/vlmathematics-6-8.

Multiple groups will be working on each object so they can compare and discuss recommendations when this information moves to the art classroom for decision making. Ms. Halstrom shows the students pictures of the various ways to attach the labels and they talk about the impact each has on the working dimensions of the sign (Figure 2.2). Then she sends them off to work in their groups.

EFFECT SIZE FOR PLANNING AND PREDICTION = 0.76

As the students work, Ms. Halstrom watches them measure and listens to the conversations each pair has. She says, "I notice you have different values in your chart here. Tell me about those differences. What do they mean?" In this case, one student is calculating using 3.14 for π, while the other is using the pi key on the calculator without rounding the result before recording it. Ms. Halstrom wants the students to discuss these two approaches and the different results they give. Prior to this lesson, Ms. Halstrom thoughtfully developed questions that would engage

OBJECTS WITH SAMPLE LABELS

a. (water cooler with sign)

Source: Allkindza/iStock.com

b. (utility pole with sign)

Source: MadCircles/iStock.com

c. (lamp post with sign)

Source: The_Life_Spectrum/iStock.com

d. (water bottle with sign)

Source: Shablon/iStock.com

e. (outdoor garbage can with sign)

Source: Nicolas McComber/iStock.com

Figure 2.2

Near transfer occurs when the new situation is paired closely with a context students have experienced.

Far transfer occurs when the learner is able to make connections between more seemingly remote situations.

Teaching Takeaway

Learners' responses to our questions are feedback on both the quality of the question and learners' level of understanding.

EFFECT SIZE FOR SELF-REGULATION STRATEGIES = 0.52

her learners in both the **near transfer** and **far transfer** of their learning. For example, she engaged several students in a dialogue around the following questions: "Show me with your hand where the label will go on the object. How wide is the label? How does that width relate to the dimensions of the cylinder?" She wanted to scaffold her learners' thinking as they engaged in far transfer—transferring their prior learning to a context more remote from the current task. With another group of learners, she supported their engagement in near transfer by asking them, "What measurement(s) do you know? What are you trying to figure out? What formula might be helpful for this?"

When they are measuring objects, learners are challenged by the more irregular shapes now before them, such as the water bottle with the angled top. This is the real world, where cylindrical objects are not perfect cylinders with straight sides and students must use some judgement. The students at first struggle to measure the diameter of objects without a visible center point. Ms. Halstrom asks the students to use their understanding of error from their science class to help them decide how to adjust their exact measurements to the number they want but cannot measure precisely. "Is there an approach to this problem that minimizes the opportunities for error in your measurements?" Eventually, one student realizes that they can measure the circumference directly for these objects in front of them. He takes the tape measure, wraps it around the body of the water bottle, and proclaims, "8¾ inches!" His partner records this on the sheet and they both pause as they realize they must still identify the diameter. Ms. Halstrom reminds her students that they know how to figure this out and walks away to talk with another group. She hears the group ask another pair about how to use the formula backward and is pleased to hear her students collaborating on this challenge.

Ms. Halstrom writes a pass and the students head outdoors with their tape measures to debate the height of signs and methods of attaching them. As Ms. Halstrom moves around the room, she is making deliberate decisions about the support she provides each pair of students. Her goal is to leave each team struggling productively about the work—considering how to respond to a question she believes they can correctly answer. The students who measured circumference and now need to calculate diameter have the tools to do that. They were not productive when they could not agree on how to begin the task, so Ms. Halstrom provided more support then.

Teaching for Clarity at the Close

With about 10 minutes left in the class, Ms. Halstrom gathers her students together to wrap up the lesson. Prior to today's lesson, she strategically matched student pairs for the wrap-up. Her decision about teams was driven by learners' readiness to communicate about their mathematics learning. For example, Cassandra is very willing to share her thinking and ask questions. She is an excellent partner to Mark, who will share his thinking when asked. In some cases, both partners might be reluctant to share their thinking. In this case, Ms. Halstrom will be close by to facilitate the conversation. Now in groups of four, learners talk through their work from the day. As learners reflect on their learning, they refer to the success criteria presented at the start of today's lesson. Ms. Halstrom encourages her learners to use the success criteria to guide their conversations. In addition to discussing the process, for example, what objects did they work with? How did they go about determining the dimensions? What challenges did they encounter in the process? How did they get around those challenges? She asks them to provide evidence that they met today's success criteria. Following the typical routine of using a different color writing utensil (e.g., colored pencil or marker), students edit their own work based on this collaborative conversation. Note that they are encouraged to do this rather than erase so that Ms. Halstrom can see the evolution of their work. They know Ms. Halstrom likes seeing how their thinking changed and they make notes to explain why they changed what they did. Ms. Halstrom will not accept "because my partner said so" as an answer, and she will ask students to explain their change in thinking. As the class ends, Ms. Halstrom collects their papers for review. These papers will serve as the exit ticket for the day, as they provide insight into her learners' thinking. She will return the papers tomorrow so students can begin to transition to the next step of the project—label design.

Ms. Halstrom was confident her students know the procedures for calculating area or circumference based on exit tickets and homework over the past several days. Today's calculations provided another opportunity to confirm that her students know how to handle the many decimal places a calculator provides and give a reasonable answer for the scale of the work. Her

Teaching Takeaway

We must use feedback from our students—in this case, the learners' conversations and actions—to adjust instruction and where we are going next.

EFFECT SIZE FOR EVALUATION AND REFLECTION = 0.75 AND METACOGNITIVE STRATEGIES = 0.60

EFFECT SIZE FOR FEEDBACK = 0.70

collaboration with the science teacher in this area is paying off in good reasoning skills for their students. She smiled as she remembered the students who measured circumference directly and then realized they still needed to find the diameter to complete the assignment. One big idea around formulas that she has been trying to impart to her students is that, as she says, "If you know some parts, you can calculate others!" This focus on flexible, algebraic thinking is imperative if students are to transfer their procedural knowledge to real-world applications. She and her students alike were pleased they met the challenge of working backward today.

Timing was as important as any other element of planning when Ms. Halstrom was designing this task. She knows that this task constitutes problem-based learning (PBL), which has a very low effect size when used as a sole means of instruction. This is because PBL is best used as a strategy for teaching for transfer, where it has higher effect size, which is exactly where her students are in their learning at this point. If students are still developing a surface-level understanding of concepts and procedures, for instance, they likely will not have access to a task such as this. The increased difficulty of each individual step could prevent them from seeing the complex connectivity between concepts.

Ms. Halstrom is pleased with how well her differentiation worked on this task. For students who still needed practice with measuring diameter, she had assigned them either the water coolers or water bottles as one of their required tasks. For students who were ready for more complexity, she had assigned the utility poles with varying diameters or the water bottle with a sloping top section. They figured out that lacing was a better means of attachment for the utility poles and settled on dimensions just smaller than the smallest possible circumference. Depending on which water cooler or water bottle a group selected, there may have been a surprise complexity element, as there was a spigot to work around on the water cooler and the sloping top of the water bottle added a height challenge. She'd heard some interesting discussions about how tall to make the signs and that pleased her. The multiple entry points and solution pathways this rich task provided worked well for Ms. Halstrom's class. Every student had applied their knowledge of circumference to solving this problem and they had persevered through the design challenge aspects of the task. Figure 2.3 shows how Ms. Halstrom made her planning visible so that she could then provide an engaging and rigorous learning experience for her learners.

EFFECT SIZE FOR PROBLEM-BASED LEARNING = 0.26

EFFECT SIZE FOR PROBLEM-BASED LEARNING = 0.61 WHEN USED FOR TRANSFER LEARNING

Teaching Takeaway

Using the right approach at the right time increases our impact on student learning in the mathematics classroom.

Ms. Halstrom's Teaching for Clarity PLANNING GUIDE

ESTABLISHING PURPOSE

1 **What are the key content standards I will focus on in this lesson?**

Content Standards:

7.G.B

Solve real-life and mathematical problems involving angle measure, area, surface area, and volume.

7.G.B.4

Know the formulas for the surface area and circumference of a circle and use them to solve problems.

Standards for Mathematical Practice:

- Make sense of problems and persevere in solving them.
- Model with mathematics.

2 **What are the learning intentions (the goal and *why* of learning, stated in student-friendly language) I will focus on in this lesson?**

Content: I am learning to apply my understanding of area and circumference of circles to surface area of cylindrical objects when deciding how large a sign or label should be.

Language: I am learning to use mathematics vocabulary (circumference, diameter, area, surface area, height) when solving problems related to cylindrical objects.

Social: I am learning to engage in productive discussions about how my peers approached their specific problem—including their reasoning and modeling of the scenario.

3 When will I introduce and reinforce the learning intention(s) so that students understand it, see the relevance, connect it to previous learning, and can clearly communicate it themselves?

At the beginning of the class, I will introduce the project by showing them several cylindrical objects (e.g., water bottles, water coolers, lamp poles, utility poles, garbage cans) and asking them how to size the labels that will go on these objects for the festival. At that point, I will introduce both the learning intentions and success criteria.

Before I distribute the label size calculations chart, I will ask my learners to relate the task to the learning intentions and success criteria. I want to eliminate any ambiguity before they begin the task.

SUCCESS CRITERIA

4 What evidence shows that students have mastered the learning intention(s)? What criteria will I use?

I can statements:

- I can calculate the circumference of a circle and the surface area of a cylinder.

- I can explain how the dimensions of a cylindrical object relate to the surface area.

- I can describe the relationship between the circumference of a circle and surface area.

- I can give appropriate dimensions for the label for each object based on the size of the object and attachment method selected.

5 How will I check students' understanding (assess learning) during instruction and make accommodations?

As students work, I will observe and listen to their partner conversations about the task. I will listen for three major elements:

- Seeing that circumference of the cylinder is also the length of the rectangular label.
- Using measurement and formulas appropriately.
- Taking the method of affixing the label into consideration of the size.

I will use the following questions to help students clarify their thinking:

- Show me with your hand where the label will go on the object. How wide is the label? How does that width relate to the dimensions of the cylinder?

- What measurement(s) do you know? What are you trying to figure out? What formula might be helpful for this?

INSTRUCTION

6 What activities and tasks will move students forward in their learning?

Students will calculate dimensions for rectangular labels/signs to be placed on cylindrical objects. They will decide how the label/sign will be placed (laced on, paper affixed with overlap) and both calculate the exact dimensions and allow for the more/less required for the method of placement.

Possible items to label include a cylindrical thermos (e.g., for drinks, like the big orange ones sports teams use), a telephone or street lamp pole (e.g., a sign for a current cause), a cylindrical garbage can (e.g., a sleeve to align with an event), or a water bottle with a sloped top (measure the right part).

After I review the task with the whole class, each pair of students will be assigned two objects to determine label size. I will differentiate the task for difficulty and complexity for students based on the objects assigned to each pair.

The telephone pole and garbage can tasks require no measurement but more visualization—this may make them more complex. The can and jar have a constant diameter and require measurement, so they are more difficult from a skill perspective. The most complex task is the water bottle because the diameter is not constant.

7   **What resources (materials and sentence frames) are needed?**

1. Student recording sheet
2. Sample objects; dimensions of larger objects
3. Measurement tools (rulers, tape measures, firm twine)
4. Calculators

8   **How will I organize and facilitate the learning? What questions will I ask? How will I initiate closure?**

1. Introduce the Task
   - Show students pictures from previous festivals and remind them that they will be designing signs in art class. Today we are figuring out the dimensions of the signs using what we have learned about circles.
   - Show samples of the various objects and review the possible ways to attach the sign or label.
   - Review the learning intentions, success criteria, and assignment sheet with the class.
   - Assign specific objects to each pair of students.
2. Partner Work
   - Students measure, calculate, and determine sign dimensions for each assigned object.
   - Students may work on additional objects as time permits.
3. Closure
   - Match two pairs of students to discuss their work. There is at least one common object between the two pairs so they can compare results as well as strategy.

online resources ↖ This lesson plan is available for download at resources.corwin.com/vlmathematics-6-8.

Figure 2.3   Ms. Halstrom's Application Lesson on Circles and Cylinders

Ms. Fernandez and Systems of Linear Equations

Ms. Fernandez is excited. Her algebra students have a conceptual under-standing and procedural knowledge of systems of linear equations and are ready to transfer their learning to new and novel situations. Over the past few weeks, her students have been solving systems of linear equations algebraically, graphing systems of equations, and using linear functions to model authentic situations. She has designed an application task that she hopes will resonate with her students as a relevant and authentic coalescing of these concepts and procedures. Today, her students are going job hunting.

APPLICATION TASK:
SCHOOL'S OUT—CLOCK IN—ROCK ON!

School is out for summer! Don't rejoice too long, because *summer fun* can come with a price tag. One of your favorite bands is coming to town during the summer and you need to buy your own ticket. The better the seat you want, the more you'll have to pay. In order to pay for your seat, you have decided to get a summer job.

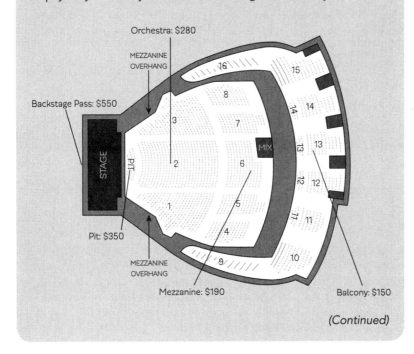

(Continued)

Video 5
Finding the Right
Application Task

https://resources.corwin.com/vlmathematics-6-8

(Continued)

The prices for different seats are shown on the venue map on the previous page. These prices are as follows:

Balcony: $150

Mezzanine: $190

Orchestra: $280

Pit: $350

Backstage Pass: $550

You have been looking at local job listings for students on summer break and found the following opportunities for work, including when they start, how much you would get paid for each day you work, and how many days you could work each week.

Job	Start Date	Daily Rate	Days per Week	Weekly Rate
Lifeguard	Week 1	$45	2	
Babysitting	Week 3	$30	4	
Dog Walking	Week 0	$15	5	
Ice Cream Server	Week 2	$40	3	
Mowing Lawns	Week 0	$50	1	

Each group will be assigned different information to fill in the following question frame for this task:

If the concert is in _____ weeks, and you want to buy the _____ ticket, which two jobs are the best to help you reach your goal? Which job is not a good option?

You will present your group's work on a collaborative poster. The poster must have four sections, one for each of today's success criteria. In each section, you will present your work demonstrating mastery on that *I can* statement. For example, the first *I can* statement is "I can mathematically model a situation with a system of linear equations." Under that section in your poster, you will need to show several linear equations: one for each of the summer jobs you are modeling, one for your ticket price, and one for your concert deadline. Each equation should be labeled to identify what each variable represents. A sample layout of this poster can be found below.

[Your Number of Weeks and Ticket Type]	
• I can mathematically model a situation with a system of linear equations. Equation for money made from Job 1 over time Equation for money made from Job 2 over time … Ticket Price: y = [Dollar Amount] Concert Deadline: x = [Week Number]	• I can solve systems of linear equations using my preferred method (algebraically or graphically). [Solve algebraically here OR Solve graphically here.]
• I can use my math as evidence to collaboratively construct a claim about a real-world situation. Based on our evidence above, we claim that the _____ job and _____ job are the best to reach our goal. On the other hand, the _____ job is not a good option to reach our goal.	• I can logically communicate how my mathematical evidence supports my claim to my peers. Our claim is supported by _____. Additionally, _____ _____

online resources — This task is available for download at resources.corwin.com/vlmathematics-6-8.

Ms. Fernandez believes that all of her learners can engage in the application of concepts and thinking skills. As a seasoned practitioner of rich and rigorous mathematics tasks, Ms. Fernandez recognizes that in the absence of access, no rigor exists. For this reason, she has delineated the various skills required for successful completion by success criteria and designed a series of scaffolds that she can use to support her learners on an "as needed" basis. Thus, she intends to maximize the rigor for each individual by differentiating the level of supports for each of her learners. These supports include, but are not limited to, manipulatives, worked examples, and access to technology. Additionally, she recognizes that mathematically modeling and deriving linear equations from a context is challenging. As eighth graders, her students are engaging in their first experiences with mathematical modeling using algebra. They have solved real-world problems using algebra, but this is one of the first tasks to ask them to return to the real-world context, make a claim, and use mathematics to justify that claim. This is why Ms. Fernandez will be starting her lesson with a teacher-facilitated close reading of the task. She wants to make sure that *every* student has the opportunity to understand the context of the task, the given information, and the goal of the task before she releases them to work collaboratively in groups. After all, if teacher clarity is essential for her students' learning, then her students should have a general sense of what they are learning, why they are learning it, and what success looks like for this particular task.

> COGNITIVE TASK
> ANALYSIS = 1.29

Application of mathematics is where the melding of ideas and skills allows us to make sense of the world around us.

What Ms. Fernandez Wants Her Students to Learn

One metaphor used to describe tasks for transfer is the active connecting from one branch of a concept map to another. This becomes abundantly clear in applied mathematics, in which very rarely is a single branch of conceptual understanding or an individual offshoot of procedural knowledge useful in isolation. Application of mathematics is where the melding of ideas and skills allows us to make sense of the world around us. This is evident in the litany of content standards typically addressed when teaching students application of mathematics, as seen below. Ms. Fernandez is focusing on the following standards:

MATHEMATICS CONTENT AND PRACTICE STANDARDS

8.EE.C.8

Analyze and solve pairs of simultaneous linear equations.

a. Understand that solutions to a system of two linear equations in two variables correspond to points of intersection of their graphs, because points of intersection satisfy both equations simultaneously.

---

b. Solve systems of two linear equations in two variables algebraically, and estimate solutions by graphing the equations. Solve simple cases by inspection. For example, $3x + 2y = 5$ and $3x + 2y = 6$ have no solution because $3x + 2y$ cannot simultaneously be 5 and 6.

c. Solve real-world and mathematical problems leading to linear equations in two variables. For example, given coordinates for two pairs of points, determine whether the line through the first pair of points intersects the line through the second pair.

8.F.B.4

Construct a function to model a linear relationship between two quantities. Determine the rate of change and initial value of the function from a description of a relationship or from two (x, y) values, including reading these from a table or from a graph. Interpret the rate of change and initial value of a linear function in terms of the situation it models, and in terms of its graph or a table of values.

Ms. Fernandez is helping her learners develop the following Standards for Mathematical Practice:

- Construct viable arguments and critique the reasoning of others.

- Look for and make use of structure.

- Reason abstractly and quantitatively.

- Model with mathematics.

Her students studied linear functions in an earlier unit, extending their Grade 7 work on linear equations. This unit has used and further developed that thinking to support new learning about systems of linear equations and the situations they represent.

Learning Intentions and Success Criteria

With her focus on the above standards, Ms. Fernandez turns her attention to making the learning visible to her students. To do this, she develops the learning intentions and success criteria for this specific application task.

Ms. Fernandez chooses to communicate the daily learning she intends for her students through content, language, and social lenses, because she finds this gives her the flexibility to target different areas of growth for different students. She also suggests that this dynamic approach helps ensure she is addressing the bigger picture of learning—like how we communicate and compare our thinking to others so we can grow further together with our students. Her learning intentions for this lesson are as follows:

Content Learning Intention: I am learning to apply my understanding of systems of linear equations to make informed decisions about a real-world problem.

Language Learning Intention: I am learning to construct viable financial arguments based on mathematical reasoning and communicate them verbally and in writing.

Social Learning Intention: I am working toward mathematical and logical consensus with my collaborative team.

Ms. Fernandez always starts her day by reviewing the learning intentions, briefly discussing them, and then referring back to them throughout the lesson to keep students progressing. She is careful not to simply use the content standard as her learning intention. Instead, she unpacks the standard and presents the learning intention in student-friendly language.

Ms. Fernandez provides learners with success criteria in the form of *I can* statements so that they may self-assess their progress toward today's learning intentions. Today, she has integrated the success criteria into the structure of the application task itself so that students may monitor both their learning progress and their progress toward task completion. The four success criteria of the day are as follows:

☐ I can mathematically model a situation with a system of linear equations.

☐ I can solve systems of linear equations using my preferred method (algebraically or graphically).

☐ I can use my math as evidence to collaboratively construct a claim about a real-world situation.

☐ I can logically communicate how my mathematical evidence supports my claim to my peers.

When applying mathematics concepts and thinking skills, it is important for students to be mindful of *what* mathematical knowledge they are drawing on and *why* they are utilizing those concepts and procedures. This metacognitive process serves as a means of grounding thinking and provides a lasting sense of direction when solving complex problems. Ms. Fernandez thinks of this process as a system of checks and balances between the specific context and the abstract mathematics. This fluid "back and forth" between the mathematics and the context is apparent in Ms. Fernandez's success criteria. The first two criteria call on a conceptual understanding of linear functions and their structure, as well as a procedural fluency with their manipulation. The last two criteria, however, are clearly asking students to investigate their ability to transfer their abstract skillset to the concrete and communicate *how* their mathematical understanding applies to this situation. By providing students with the means to self-assess against these measures, Ms. Fernandez is providing students a scaffold toward metacognition. In addition, the success criteria align with the learning intentions to be sure and offer learners an opportunity to engage in content, language, and social learning.

> EFFECT SIZE FOR METACOGNITIVE STRATEGIES = 0.60

Guiding and Scaffolding Student Thinking

In this application lesson where students will be consolidating previously learned material, Ms. Fernandez intends to jump directly into guided practice with a structured close reading. She begins her day by distributing the task, *School's Out—Clock In—Rock On!*, to each group and instructing them to "read with a pencil" as they try to answer the question, "What is the big idea of the text?" Her students recognize this sense-making protocol as one of annotating the text in search of the overarching theme, identifying phrases or words they do not yet understand, and locating key details that might help them in their work.

Teaching Takeaway

Text-dependent questioning can guide students to identify key details and make inferences in mathematics.

Text-dependent questions are questions that are answered through close reading, requiring learners to use evidence from the text. These questions should encourage understanding beyond the recall of basic facts.

Focusing questions allow students to do the cognitive work of learning by helping to push their thinking forward.

Funneling questions guide students down the teacher's path to find the answer.

TEXT-DEPENDENT QUESTIONS

☐ What is the big idea of the task/text? What are we doing?

☐ What is the *mezzanine* section? What is a *backstage pass*? How does the venue map help make sense of the ticket prices?

☐ How do ticket prices play a role in the task?

☐ What information is provided in the table? What does each column mean? What does each row mean?

☐ What exactly *is* "Daily Rate"? Why is this information important to the task?

☐ What are the questions we are ultimately trying to answer through this task?

☐ What are some initial ideas about how we might use math to approach this task?

☐ How might a system of linear equations help us?

☐ How can we use the information in the table to create linear equations? What would *y*-values represent? What would *x*-values represent?

☐ How can we determine the *weekly rate* for each job?

☐ How do the *start dates* factor into creating linear equations?

This strategy of **text-dependent questioning** is intended to guide students from the broad peripherals of a text, where a general understanding can be gained, down to specific sections and key details where inferences can be drawn. You will notice that Ms. Fernandez employs both *focusing* and *funneling* types of text-dependent questions (Herbel-Eisenmann & Breyfogle, 2005; Wood, 1998). Her general strategy is to start with a prompting **focusing question**, and then cue her students with a **funneling question** if they need an extra boost or are not quite getting where she intends for them to go. Again, her goal is to maintain the maximum rigor for each student while ensuring access for all. Ms. Fernandez reflects on her approach:

> I remember when I was a student, my teacher would read these problems, do all of the setup, and point out what the problem was asking of us. We just had to perform the calculations. As a beginning teacher, I did much the same thing, but eventually realized that in helping my students just "get to the math" I was actually doing all the thinking for them. I want my students to understand what the task is asking of them, but I want them to see that it involves more than just plugging in numbers and getting an answer. I want them to be able to apply their understanding to problems in the future, especially when those problems are outside of the classroom.

Now, Ms. Fernandez has learned to scaffold, rather than eliminate, the complexity of inferencing mathematics from a situation.

As her students finish their close reading and embark on the rest of the task in their groups, Ms. Fernandez circulates throughout the room, eavesdropping on conversations and listening carefully to make sure students are on the right track. Collaborative groups have been constructed so that students early in their English development have been paired with others who are bilingual in English and their first language (when available) so that all students may thoroughly discuss the task. Ms. Fernandez's years of experience have helped her develop a tolerance for allowing students to struggle, largely because she has learned to differentiate between productive and unproductive failure and success (Figure 2.4).

Ms. Fernandez notices one group debating over whether the *start date* of each job constitutes an *x*- or *y*-intercept. Even though she overhears some group members making inaccurate suggestions, she recognizes that one group member is respectfully disagreeing (for the right reasons) and silently nods to him approvingly. She is confident that this silent approval will empower the young man to keep advocating for his (accurate) perspective.

As she listens in on another group, however, Ms. Fernandez notices something different. This second group's conversation is notably mum compared to other groups and they seem to be stalled out. With a quick group interview she discovers that they are only able to gather that the

---

Teaching Takeaway

Providing opportunities for learners to take ownership of their learning is essential in building assessment-capable visible learners in mathematics.

> EFFECT SIZE FOR SCAFFOLDING = 0.82

> EFFECT SIZE FOR SMALL-GROUP LEARNING = 0.47

This is a student-led approach to teaching and learning mathematics.

> EFFECT SIZE FOR CLASSROOM DISCUSSION = 0.82

FOUR POSSIBLE LEARNING EVENTS

	Unproductive Failure	Unproductive Success	Productive Success	Productive Failure
Type of learning event	Unguided problem solving without further instruction	Rote memorization without conceptual understanding	Guided problem solving using prior knowledge and tasks planned for success	Unsuccessful or suboptimal problem solving using prior knowledge, followed by further instruction
Learning outcome	Frustration that leads to abandoning learning	Completion of the task without understanding its purpose or relevance	Consolidation of learning through scaffolded practice	Learning from errors and ensuring learners persist in generating and exploring representations and solutions
Useful for . . .			Surface learning of new knowledge firmly anchored to prior knowledge	Deep learning and transfer of knowledge
Undermines . . .	Agency and motivation	Goal setting and willingness to seek challenge		
Promotes . . .			Skill development and concept attainment	Use of cognitive, metacognitive, and affective strategies

Source: Frey, Hattie, & Fisher (2018).

Figure 2.4

 This chart is available for download at resources.corwin.com/vlmathematics-6-8.

Video 6
Differentiating in an Application Lesson

https://resources.corwin.com/
vlmathematics-6-8

weekly rate, which they calculated correctly for each job, is supposed to be the slope for each of their linear equations, but they are unsure of where to go from there. As Ms. Fernandez starts to prompt and eventually cue the students toward using the point-slope form of a linear equation, she recognizes that she is getting very limited acknowledgement of understanding. Since this group seems to be struggling more seriously with the concept of mathematically modeling this situation and the subsequent procedure that supports it, Ms. Fernandez decides to provide them some preprinted scaffolds specific for this part of the task. She says, "I notice that you have encountered a challenge with your conversions. How could you use this information to get around this apparent impasse?" On these printed scaffolds, the group finds a detailed procedure for converting *daily rate* and *days per week* into *weekly rate* and then utilizing *weekly rate* as slope, as well as converting *start date* into a point of the form (*week number*, 0). With this helping hand, the group is now able to access the task and begins mirroring the procedure with their own values. Before she moves on, Ms. Fernandez overhears the group start to make predictions about which jobs could make them the money they need in time for the concert based on their in-progress calculations. She recognizes their prediction as a resurfacing of their conceptual understanding of the underlying mathematics and is confident they will continue to make progress without her. To document learning, Ms. Fernandez utilizes her observation recording tool (Figure 2.5). This allows her to document progress and track who she has observed during the lesson.

Teaching for Clarity at the Close

The class periods at Ms. Fernandez's school are only a short 48 minutes in duration. Therefore, she is comfortable scheduling rich application tasks over multiple class periods. This particular task is slated to take two periods and day one ends right on schedule—students are almost done with their posters. As a quick exit ticket, she asks her learners to summarize the day on an index card using the following questions: What it is that we are learning? How did today move your learning forward? What did you do, and what did you learn? Taking note of where her learners are in their progress toward the learning intentions and success criteria, Ms. Fernandez knows where to begin on day two of this application task. She launches day two with a brief set of questions designed to quickly refresh students' thinking and get them back up to speed with the context and goal of the task. These questions are similar to yesterday's exit ticket: "With your neighbors, review what it is that we are learning. How did yesterday move your learning forward? What did you do, and what did you learn? What is your plan for today?" Students then spend about 15 minutes completing their posters and displaying them on the classroom walls. Now they are ready for a gallery walk.

Gallery walks are an efficient way for students to review their peers' work, leave feedback, and gather talking points for whole-class discussions. Students move in groups from poster to poster, briefly discussing what

SMALL-GROUP LEARNING: IMPLEMENTATION AND RECORDING TOOL FOR OBSERVATIONS

Intent of the Observation	Brief Description/Comments	Observed?
Mathematics content		
Mathematical practices or processes		
Student engagement		
General comment:		
Feedback to students:		

Source: Fennell, F., Kobett, B., & Wray, J. (2015). Classroom-based formative assessments: Guiding teaching and learning. In C. Suurtamm (Ed.) & A. R. McDuffie (Series Ed.), *Annual perspectives in mathematics education: Assessment to enhance teaching and learning* (pp. 51–62). Reston, VA: National Council of Teachers of Mathematics. Republished with permission of the National Council of Teachers of Mathematics.

Figure 2.5

online resources This template is available for download at resources.corwin.com/vlmathematics-6-8.

they see, leaving comments for the authors on sticky notes, and recording notes of their own. As the students in Ms. Fernandez's class go about their rotations, Ms. Fernandez is thrilled to hear them making connections between their own work and the work of their peers. Groups end their rotations by revisiting their own posters and discussing the feedback from other groups. As before, Ms. Fernandez eavesdrops on these conversations and uses her observation recording tool to document the evidence.

Ms. Fernandez closes the task and application lesson by leading a discussion with her whole class. She revisits the learning intentions and success criteria to open the discussion and then begins asking questions. She strategically groups her questions and delivers them in a specific order, starting with a series of conclusion or *what's the answer* questions. Through these she is able to formatively assess the overall impact of the task.

Conclusion Questions:

- What did we discover? Which jobs were the best for your situation?

- How does your math justify your claim?

She then moves on to process questions that assess students' ability to apply their mathematics. She wants to know if students are internalizing the "nuts and bolts" of how they came to their conclusions. Can they re-justify their claims, if needed? Students' answers to these structural questions hold implications to their ability to transfer this specific application to additional situations.

Process Questions:

- What did we need *mathematically* in order to investigate this situation?

- Why/how do these equations represent the money made from each job over time?

- What was the point of solving a system of equations? What does the solution represent?

- How did your group decide to solve your system? Why?

- What other situations might lend themselves to this type of modeling?

Gallery walks are an efficient way for students to review their peers' work, leave feedback, and gather talking points for whole-class discussions.

EFFECT SIZE FOR
SUMMARIZATION
= 0.79

EFFECT SIZE FOR
QUESTIONING
= 0.48

She concludes with a set of reflection questions designed to make students extend their thinking beyond the rigidity of their calculations. These questions are intended to help the task make a lasting impression on students and "keep them thinking" as they leave class. She is hoping to activate those checks and balances between the concrete context and the abstract mathematics within her students and generate a desire to "tinker" with their models, as this iterative process of refinement is truly the role of applied mathematicians.

EFFECT SIZE FOR EVALUATION AND REFLECTION = 0.75

Reflection Questions:

- What possible inaccuracies exist in our assumptions/generalizations? Where is our math the weakest?
- Could anything change our claims (e.g., different job start dates, different number of days worked per week, rainy days or getting sent home from work early, working more than one job, etc.)?
- Overall, how confident are we in our claims?

Video 7
Facilitating and Evaluating Learning in an Application Lesson

https://resources.corwin.com/ vlmathematics-6-8

This application task was the result of specific, intentional, and purposeful decisions about mathematics instruction critical for student growth and achievement. Although the outcome of these decisions is shared here, the process for arriving at this point originated from Ms. Fernandez's focus during the planning process. Figure 2.6 shows how Ms. Fernandez made her planning visible so that she could then provide an engaging and rigorous learning experience for her learners.

Ms. Fernandez's Teaching for Clarity PLANNING GUIDE

ESTABLISHING PURPOSE

1

What are the key content standards I will focus on in this lesson?

Content Standards:

8.EE.C.8

Analyze and solve pairs of simultaneous linear equations.

a. Understand that solutions to a system of two linear equations in two variables correspond to points of intersection of their graphs, because points of intersection satisfy both equations simultaneously.

b. Solve systems of two linear equations in two variables algebraically, and estimate solutions by graphing the equations. Solve simple cases by inspection. For example, $3x + 2y = 5$ and $3x + 2y = 6$ have no solution because $3x + 2y$ cannot simultaneously be 5 and 6.

c. Solve real-world and mathematical problems leading to linear equations in two variables. For example, given coordinates for two pairs of points, determine whether the line through the first pair of points intersects the line through the second pair.

8.F.B.4

Construct a function to model a linear relationship between two quantities. Determine the rate of change and initial value of the function from a description of a relationship or from two (x,y) values, including reading these from a table or from a graph. Interpret the rate of change and initial value of a linear function in terms of the situation it models, and in terms of its graph or a table of values.

Standards for Mathematical Practice:

- *Construct viable arguments and critique the reasoning of others.*
- *Look for and make use of structure.*
- *Reason abstractly and quantitatively.*
- *Model with mathematics.*

2   What are the learning intentions (the goal and *why* of learning, stated in student-friendly language) I will focus on in this lesson?

Content: I am learning to apply my understanding of systems of linear equations to make informed decisions about a real-world problem.

Language: I am learning to construct viable financial arguments based on mathematical reasoning and communicate them verbally and in writing.

Social: I am working toward mathematical and logical consensus with my collaborative team.

3   When will I introduce and reinforce the learning intention(s) so that students understand it, see the relevance, connect it to previous learning, and can clearly communicate it themselves?

I will open the day with an overview to set the stage for this closing transfer task ("We've gained all these tools. Let's put them to use together to solve real-world problems"). As I introduce the task, I will refer back to the learning intentions and make connections to activate students' prior knowledge (i.e., remind them about how they can model situations with linear functions when discussing the context of the task; remind them how they can solve systems of linear equations algebraically and graphically and how to interpret a solution given a context, etc.).

As students engage in the task, I will refer to the language intention to stimulate the use of academic and content language in their speaking and writing. I will refer to the social intention to remind students of our expectations of collaboration and building consensus based on mathematical evidence.

SUCCESS CRITERIA

4 What evidence shows that students have mastered the learning intention(s)? What criteria will I use?

I can statements:

- *I can mathematically model a situation with a system of linear equations.*
- *I can solve systems of linear equations using my preferred method (algebraically or graphically).*
- *I can use my math as evidence to collaboratively construct a claim about a real-world situation.*
- *I can logically communicate how my mathematical evidence supports my claim to my peers.*

5 How will I check students' understanding (assess learning) during instruction and make accommodations?

We will begin the day with a structured close read of the task itself to ensure all students come to a shared understanding of the context and what the problem is asking. Students will be asked to re-voice the context of the task and the end goal of the task with their groups, and each group will be asked to share with the whole class. This is where we will discuss any unclear content and academic language. This is especially important for our ELLs, who will be encouraged to use their personal electronic devices or school devices to help translate unfamiliar English words to their first language. Additionally, collaborative groups have been constructed with this in mind—students early in their English development have been paired with others who are bilingual in English and their first language (when available) so that all students may thoroughly discuss the task.

Once students start digging into the task collaboratively, I will scan the classroom, table to table, listening in on conversations and redirecting as needed. I will be careful not to interfere while students are productively struggling through the intended rigor of the task, but only step in when groups seem to be at a dead end. Based on the reason for their stalled production, I have a series of predesigned scaffolds at the ready.

INSTRUCTION

6 What activities and tasks will move students forward in their learning?

Collaborative Task: School's Out-Clock In-Rock On!

This close-reading application task leads to a collaborative poster followed by a gallery walk and whole-class discussion.

7 What resources (materials and sentence frames) are needed?

1. *Printed copies of the task for each learner*
2. *Sticky poster paper for collaborative posters*
3. *Markers for posters*
4. *Printed copies of Scaffold 1-Parallel problem turning the given information (start date, daily rate, days worked per week) into the slope of a line (weekly rate) and the start date into the x-intercept of the form (week number, 0).*
5. *Printed copies of Scaffold 2-Review of solving systems of linear equations with references to prior class notes and examples.*

8 How will I organize and facilitate the learning? What questions will I ask? How will I initiate closure?

1. *Close Reading (Whole-Class)/Text-Dependent Questions*

   - *What is the big idea of the task/text? What are we doing?*
   - *What is the mezzanine section? What is a backstage pass? How does the venue map help make sense of the ticket prices?*
   - *How do ticket prices play a role in the task?*
   - *What information is provided in the table? What does each column mean? What does each row mean?*
   - *What exactly is "Daily Rate"? Why is this information important to the task?*
   - *What are the questions we are ultimately trying to answer through this task?*

- What are some initial ideas about how we might use math to approach this task?
- How might a system of linear equations help us?
- How can we use the information in the table to create linear equations? What would y-values represent? What would x-values represent?
- How can we determine the weekly rate for each job?
- How do the start dates factor into creating linear equations?

2. Collaborative Work/Guided Practice

Once the class as a whole understands the context and goal of the task via the close reading, I will release them to work collaboratively. This will be my opportunity to engage struggling groups in guided practice around the necessary computations to keep the task moving forward. This is also the time for formative scanning and eavesdropping.

3. Gallery Walk

Completed posters will be displayed around the room. Groups will cycle through the room, poster to poster, leaving feedback on sticky notes and gathering talking points for the upcoming whole-class conversation.

4. Wrap-Up/Whole-Class Discussion (Backward questioning)

Conclusion

- What did we discover? Which jobs were the best for your situation?
- How does your math justify your claim?

Process

- What did we need mathematically in order to investigate this situation?
- Why/how do these equations represent the money made from each job over time?
- What was the point of solving a system of equations? What does the solution represent?

- *How did your group decide to solve your system? Why?*
- *What other situations might lend themselves to this type of modeling?*

Reflection

- *What possible inaccuracies exist in our assumptions/ generalizations? Where is our math the weakest?*
- *Could anything change our claims (e.g., different job start dates, different number of days worked per week, rainy days or getting sent home from work early, working more than one job, etc.)?*
- *Overall, how confident are we in our claims?*

online resources — This lesson plan is available for download at resources.corwin.com/vlmathematics-6-8.

Figure 2.6   Ms. Fernandez's Application Lesson on Systems of Linear Equations

A **classroom challenge** (CC) is a classroom-ready lesson that supports formative assessment. CCs help teachers assess and improve students' understanding of mathematical concepts and skills and their ability to use mathematical practices or processes. See http://map.mathshell.org.uk/materials/lessons.php.

Moving from algebra to integers, let us look at a different way of teaching the application of concepts and thinking skills in the Visible Learning classroom.

Mr. Singh and Integers

Integers are a major unit of study in Mr. Singh's sixth grade class. Because his current state standards include understanding both integers and integer operations, students have learned a wide range of mathematical ideas associated with this subset of real numbers. He wants to understand what his students have mastered and where their remaining misconceptions are around integer comparison, addition, and subtraction. While most students are able to add or subtract two integers accurately when given a computation task, Mr. Singh is not certain students have transferred their understanding of addition and subtraction problem structures to the context of integers. He finds **classroom challenges** to be a powerful tool in his classroom and has chosen to implement a **concept development lesson**, *Using Positive and Negative Numbers in Context* (Shell Center for Mathematical Education, 2015) today to provide students an opportunity to apply the mathematics they have learned to temperature change situations and to assess their understanding. This will provide Mr. Singh with the information he needs to solidify important learning and resolve misconceptions before the class moves to multiplication and division of integers.

In deciding on this particular resource (*Using Positive and Negative Numbers in Context*), he did not simply use an Internet search engine to find "cool" activities related to integers. Instead, he devoted a significant amount of time to answer the guiding questions that support planning for clarity (see Figure I.5) and then found the resource on a well-vetted web resource site. Before he even began his search for resources, Mr. Singh was clear about what he wanted his students to learn, what evidence would show that his students had learned the specific content, and how he would monitor their learning. Let us take a closer look at his learning intentions and success criteria.

What Mr. Singh Wants His Students to Learn

Mr. Singh wants his students to apply their conceptual understanding and procedural skills with integers to authentic contexts and scenarios. At the same time, he wants to engage his learners in an application task that also makes their thinking visible so that he can identify any gaps in their conceptual understanding and procedural knowledge. For example, in the application of integers, Mr. Singh would like to make sure his learners are both confident and strong in ordering, comparing, adding, and subtracting positive and negative numbers. The specific application task must assimilate those concepts and skills.

This lesson reflects a balance of conceptual understanding (how integers reflect directional change in value), procedural fluency (computing missing values), and application (solving a collection of problems around temperature change) within a single experience. Although he was educated under the idea that rigor means doing more problems faster or working with larger numbers, Mr. Singh now understands mathematical rigor in the context of this balance of conceptual understanding, procedural fluency, and application across a curriculum because his

A **concept development lesson** supports learners in refining their conceptual understanding of a concept and then applying that concept to new situations. Concept development lessons are meant to first reveal students' prior knowledge and then develop students' understanding of important mathematical ideas, connecting concepts to other mathematical knowledge.

EFFECT SIZE FOR SELF-EFFICACY = 0.92

EFFECT SIZE FOR CONCENTRATION/ PERSISTENCE/ ENGAGEMENT = 0.56

mathematics specialist training was enlightening. It gave him permission to spend more time developing his students' deep understanding of mathematics as a well-rounded discipline. Although procedural fluency matters (e.g., his students must be able to compute fluently with integers), it also matters that his students understand what integers are and how they are used in a variety of settings. The primary purpose of today's lesson is to apply integer addition and subtraction in the context of temperature change. This lesson addresses two parts of one content standard and focuses on the process standard of problem solving.

MATHEMATICS CONTENT AND PRACTICE STANDARDS

Virginia Standard of Learning 6.6

The student will

a. add, subtract, multiply, and divide integers; and

b. solve practical problems involving operations with integers; and

c. simplify numerical expressions involving integers.

Mr. Singh is helping his learners develop the following Virginia Mathematical Process Goal for Students:

- Mathematical problem solving

Learning Intentions and Success Criteria

As is his practice, Mr. Singh goes beyond listing the standards addressed in the lesson because the standards have remained the same for most of the unit but the intent of each lesson is much more specific. His learning intentions for today's lesson are as follows:

Content Learning Intention: I am learning to use my understanding of integer addition and subtraction to solve problems about temperature comparisons or changes.

Language Learning Intention: I am learning to explain my problem-solving approach verbally and in writing.

Social Learning Intention: I am learning to explain my problem-solving thinking clearly to my peers.

Mr. Singh understands that his students perform best when they have a clear picture of what success looks like. At the beginning of Grade 6, he introduces this idea with a travel analogy. He shows students pictures of iconic locations in the United States and asks them about taking a road trip (Figure 2.7).

Mr. Singh asks, "If you're headed to New York City, how will you know when you've arrived? Which sight will you see? What if you're going to St. Louis?" Moving to math, he asks how students know they can add fractions or multiply whole numbers. This starts a discussion of success criteria and how important they are to learning. For this lesson, Mr. Singh has identified several success criteria:

- ☐ I can find and explain temperature relationships among the cities in the task.
- ☐ I can compute missing values accurately.
- ☐ I can explain the process used to figure out missing values.

He will share these with students as part of beginning the lesson. These success criteria will be the road map for the day as students work.

Guiding and Scaffolding Student Thinking

Two days earlier, Mr. Singh used a few minutes at the end of class to give his students a preassessment task for today's lesson. He has reviewed students' work and assigned them to work in pairs on today's task based on their understanding shown on the preassessment. For this task, each student is paired with another student who performed

ICONIC LOCATIONS IN THE UNITED STATES

Sources: Statue of Liberty: FrankRamspott/iStock.com; St. Louis Arch: pseudodaemon/iStock.com

Figure 2.7

A **low floor/high ceiling task** is a task that is accessible to all learners. These tasks can be easily differentiated so that learners can engage in the task at their own level (Youcubed, 2014).

at a similar level or showed similar misconceptions. Because Mr. Singh knows that tracking students (long-term, fixed ability-grouping) is not effective, he deliberately forms groups using a variety of strategies throughout a given unit of study. For this particular activity, he wants students to work through their misconceptions with another student who shares similar thinking. Mr. Singh notices some surprises as he looks at student work, finding some students he thought were performing well who are struggling to connect integer computation with situations around temperature change. Although his lessons have included temperature and other contexts for operations, it is clear that some students still need additional experience and support. Today's task is a **low floor/high task**. He is confident every student pair will be able to begin (the low floor) by creating a trio of two city cards along with a temperature change arrow card showing the relationship (see Figure 2.8).

CITY PAIRS AND TEMPERATURE CHANGE

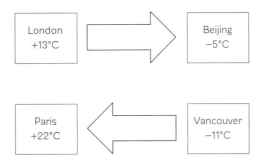

London
+13°C

Beijing
−5°C

Paris
+22°C

Vancouver
−11°C

Source: © 2015 MARS, Shell Center, University of Nottingham

Figure 2.8

Ultimately, the set of cards and arrows forms a network of cities with many different temperature relationships. Mr. Singh believes some pairs of students might complete the task but many students will not (the high ceiling).

As students enter the class, Mr. Singh uses a seating plan on the screen to direct students to sit in pairs based on their work on the preassessment. He shares the day's learning intentions and introduces the lesson. In the task, most of the arrows will include information about a city pair (e.g., travel from London to Beijing). There will be missing information for each trio (two cities and the corresponding arrow). Students must find the missing values and tell the computation they used to calculate these values. Mr. Singh asks, "Does the temperature increase or decrease as you travel from London to Beijing? How much does it change? How do you know?" He walks the class through the process of determining the direction of change, the amount of change, and the computation needed to calculate these values for each of the two examples on the screen.

Once students understand what they're supposed to do, Mr. Singh gives each pair two card sets (a collection of city cards and a collection of arrow cards, each with some temperature values provided and others missing). Students also have a paper thermometer (a vertical number line) available to support their thinking on the task. Following the

EFFECT SIZE FOR SMALL-GROUP LEARNING = 0.47

EFFECT SIZE FOR TRACKING/ STREAMING = 0.12

EFFECT SIZE FOR METACOGNITIVE STRATEGIES = 0.60

EFFECT SIZE FOR WORKED EXAMPLES = 0.37

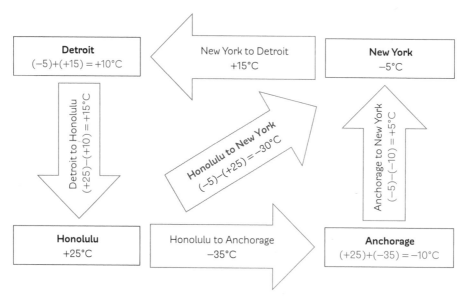

Source: Adapted from © 2015 MARS, Shell Center, University of Nottingham

Figure 2.9

Video 8
Consolidating Deep and
Transfer Learning in an
Application Lesson

https://resources.corwin.com/
vlmathematics-6-8

structure provided in the lesson, he encourages students to start finding relationships and building a network of cities. In Figure 2.9, we see an excerpt from the end result of this task—learners using the arrow cards to find the temperature of the corresponding city. For example, knowing the temperature in New York, learners will take the arrow comparing New York to Detroit and calculate the temperature in Detroit based on the arrow's information.

As Mr. Singh circulates while students work, he listens to their explanations and discussions. He sees one pair of students using the thermometer to help them calculate the temperature change from Honolulu to Anchorage: "The temperature is going down because the negative number means it is colder. It takes 25 degrees to go from +25 to zero degrees. Then there are 10 more to go because the change is 35 degrees down." These students are on a productive path, so Mr. Singh keeps moving.

Another group is struggling to find the temperature in Detroit based on the information given. One student insists that Detroit must be colder than New York (see the top row of Figure 2.9), while his partner argues that the temperature change of +15 means Detroit is warmer. Mr. Singh pauses here to ask the team some questions about the signs of the numbers and the direction of movement on the thermometer given those signs. One of the reasons he enjoys these lessons is that they are consistent with his beliefs about purposeful questioning. He has planned some questions to guide students' thinking based on the class's performance on the preassessment. His questions are focusing questions, designed to move students forward in their thinking without leading them down a teacher-determined path. For example, he might ask students to explain why they set up an equation the way they have or what the various "–" and "+" symbols mean in an equation, both as signs for numbers and as an operation. Mr. Singh always asks his students to explain their thinking. At the beginning of the year, this surprises some students and they believe their answers are wrong. As they learn more about Mr. Singh's expectations, they realize he asks because he wants to understand their thinking and he will ask whether their work is right or wrong.

EFFECT SIZE FOR QUESTIONING = 0.48

EFFECT SIZE FOR SELF-VERBALIZATION AND SELF-QUESTIONING = 0.55

Mr. Singh knows the task is challenging enough to provide a productive struggle for every student in the class. Learners who are still mastering the content may not complete the entire task, but their reasoning and problem-solving skills are challenged by the parts of the task they complete. Learners who are more advanced will progress further into the task and identify some of the more complex missing value calculations. Because the pairs of students are working at a similar level, each team is able to progress at an appropriate level of struggle while all are engaged in a rigorous problem-solving task. Mr. Singh provides glue and poster paper for students to create a poster with their cards as they work through the task. Later in the task, he encourages pairs to compare their work to that of those around them as another tool for developing their thinking. This is a variation on a gallery walk; in this case, one member of each pair switches places to ask a question of the other team about their work so far. Then the partners return to their home station to use this learning to continue their own progress.

EFFECT SIZE FOR STRATEGY MONITORING = 0.58

EFFECT SIZE FOR SEEKING HELP FROM PEERS = 0.83

Teaching for Clarity at the Close

Mr. Singh includes slides and questions to guide a whole-class discussion. He leads his class through this discussion to continue developing

Effective formative assessment can include observations, interviews, "Show me" moments that ask learners to show what they know, hinge questions, and exit tasks.

EFFECT SIZE FOR DELIBERATE PRACTICE = 0.79

their thinking in conversation with the entire class. At the end of the lesson, he gives his students a postassessment similar to the preassessment used to determine student pairs in the lesson.

The exit tasks are similar to the card sort in the lesson and ask students to work individually on similar reasoning and computation. Mr. Singh sorts student work on the postassessment into four categories, using the same criteria he used to sort the preassessment. He identifies progress in the understanding of his students as he sees the distribution of scores shift from preassessment to postassessment. When Mr. Singh reviews student work on the activity (looking at student posters) and on the postassessment, he makes notes about which students need additional learning experiences around these aspects of integer concepts and skills. His team's weekly routine includes regular time for intervention support. Mr. Singh plans to pull together small groups of students during this time so he can continue developing their skills while the class moves forward with their study of integers into multiplication and division.

As Mr. Singh reflects on the performance of his students, two specific challenges stand out. First, he noticed that many struggling learners were simply adding the two numbers given to find the missing term without thinking through the relationship among the values. Figure 2.10 shows an example of where this thinking occurred.

SITUATION WHERE SOME STUDENTS STRUGGLED TO SEE A RELATIONSHIP

Source: Adapted from © 2015 MARS, Shell Center, University of Nottingham

Figure 2.10

Here, the temperature in the two cities is given and students were asked to figure out the change in temperature when traveling from London to Beijing. One way to approach this is to create an equation reading +13 + ___ = –5. This would be read verbally as "the temperature in London, positive 13 degrees, changed by some amount, gives the temperature in Beijing, negative 5 degrees." Rather than thinking about a story with a beginning, change, and ending, however, Mr. Singh noticed that some students would add +13 to –5 and complete the blank with +8 degrees. These students struggled to apply their computation in context, not considering a question like "Does it make sense that an 8-degree temperature change represents the change in temperature from London (+13) to Beijing (–5)?" Mr. Singh can see that these students can compute correctly with integers; they find the correct solution to their incorrect equations. These students need to develop their conceptual understanding of the situations represented by addition and subtraction so they can use their procedural knowledge correctly. They do not use different strategies to find the solution depending on where the missing term is in the equation. This is what Mr. Singh will work on during intervention time.

The other common challenge Mr. Singh noticed is that his more advanced students struggled with the arrows, which included an equation but not a city pair. In the partial solution shown in Figure 2.9, this is the Honolulu to New York arrow. While they could reason about how to calculate the missing term in problems like the example above, the more complex problem of working backward from computation to situation was challenging. Although these students do not need remedial support, they will benefit from additional practice moving from symbolic representations to contextual representations. Because every student on the team participates in the intervention time, Mr. Singh can use this time to give these students this experience. This **deliberate practice** has provided the foundation for today's application task. He will also build practice on this skill into the class's work with integer multiplication and division. Figure 2.11 shows how Mr. Singh made his planning visible so that he could then provide an engaging and rigorous learning experience for his learners.

> **Deliberate practice** is the type of practice that is purposefully designed to either address particular learning gaps or refine high-level skills.

> EFFECT SIZE FOR DELIBERATE PRACTICE = 0.79

Mr. Singh's Teaching for Clarity PLANNING GUIDE

ESTABLISHING PURPOSE

1

What are the key content standards I will focus on in this lesson?

Content Standards (2016 Virginia SOLs):

Virginia Standard of Learning 6.6

The student will

a. add, subtract, multiply, and divide integers; and

b. solve practical problems involving operations with integers; and

c. simplify numerical expressions involving integers.

Mathematical Process Goal for Students:

- Mathematical problem solving

2

What are the learning intentions (the goal and *why* of learning, stated in student-friendly language) I will focus on in this lesson?

Content: I am learning to use my understanding of integer addition and subtraction to solve problems about temperature comparisons or changes.

Language: I am learning to explain my problem-solving approach verbally and in writing.

Social: I am learning to explain my problem-solving thinking clearly to my peers.

3

When will I introduce and reinforce the learning intention(s) so that students understand it, see the relevance, connect it to previous learning, and can clearly communicate it themselves?

I will introduce the lesson by providing an example of temperature change during travel. In Virginia's January winter, the temperature is quite cold. If I travel to Australia's January summer, the temperature is warmer. I can use integers to show this change with an equation. I will then share the learning intentions and success criteria for the day and provide a worked example for the task at hand.

SUCCESS CRITERIA

4 **What evidence shows that students have mastered the learning intention(s)? What criteria will I use?**

I can statements:

- I can find and explain temperature relationships among the cities in the task.
- I can compute missing values accurately.
- I can explain the process used to figure out missing values.

5 **How will I check students' understanding (assess learning) during instruction and make accommodations?**

While observing student pair progress through the task, I will pay close attention to the strategy they use to find the temperature in the corresponding city.

As learners engage in conversation and work on the task, I will ask probing questions to push their thinking forward.

INSTRUCTION

6 **What activities and tasks will move students forward in their learning?**

This will be a concept development lesson. I will pair learners based on preassessment data from the previous day. In their pairs, students will engage in a series of problems that require them to find the temperature of a city based on how much the temperature differs from another city.

7 **What resources (materials and sentence frames) are needed?**

Preassessment

1. Activity cards
2. Thermometer strips

Postassessment/exit ticket

1. Poster paper and glue sticks for recording the final network

8   How will I organize and facilitate the learning? What questions will I ask? How will I initiate closure?

1. Lesson Introduction

   I will introduce the lesson by providing an example of temperature change during travel. In Virginia's January winter, the temperature is quite cold. If I travel to Australia's January summer, the temperature is warmer. I can use integers to show this change with an equation. I will then share the learning intentions and success criteria for the day and provide a worked example for the task at hand.

2. Student Partner Work

   Students work in pairs based on preassessment performance. As learners engage in conversation and work on the task, I will ask probing questions to push their thinking forward. Student pairs will build a poster of their temperature relationship network as they identify the relationships and missing values using their knowledge of integer addition and subtraction.

3. Lesson Closure

   Near the end of the lesson, students will swap one partner with another team nearby to ask questions about their work. Then the students will bring this thinking back to their own team to continue refining their work.

   At the end of class, I will have students model their current thinking about sample problems in another whole-class discussion. The lesson ends with a brief postassessment.

 This lesson plan is available for download at resources.corwin.com/vlmathematics-6-8.

Figure 2.11   Mr. Singh's Application Lesson on Integers

Reflection

The three examples from Ms. Halstrom, Ms. Fernandez, and Mr. Singh exemplify what teaching mathematics for application of concepts and thinking skills in the Visible Learning classroom looks like. Using what you have read in this chapter, reflect on the following questions:

1. In your own words, describe what teaching for the application of concepts and thinking skills looks like in your mathematics classroom.

2. How does the Teaching for Clarity Planning Guide support your intentionality in teaching for the application of concepts and thinking skills?

3. Compare and contrast the approaches to teaching taken by the classroom teachers featured in this chapter.

4. How did the classroom teachers featured in this chapter adjust the difficulty and/or complexity of the mathematics tasks to meet the needs of all learners?

TEACHING FOR CONCEPTUAL UNDERSTANDING

3

CHAPTER 3 SUCCESS CRITERIA:

(1) I can describe what teaching for conceptual understanding in the mathematics classroom looks like.

(2) I can apply the Teaching for Clarity Planning Guide to teaching for conceptual understanding.

(3) I can compare and contrast different approaches to teaching for conceptual understanding with teaching for application.

(4) I can give examples of how to differentiate mathematics tasks designed for conceptual understanding.

In Chapter 2, we visited three classrooms as they engaged in the application of concepts and thinking skills. As you recall, the applications of mathematics to designing a label for a cylindrical object, evaluating the value of a summer job, and determining the differences in temperatures required learners to have foundational knowledge in conceptual understanding and procedural knowledge. In this chapter, we will turn back time to see how each of the three teachers, as well as the teachers featured in the videos that accompany this book, supported their learners as they developed conceptual understanding in their mathematics learning.

If learners are to see mathematics as more than algorithms and mnemonics, we must provide learning experiences that focus on the underlying properties and principles. For Ms. Halstrom, Ms. Fernandez, and Mr. Singh, the end goal is to understand, conceptually, area and circumference, systems of equations, and integers. All three teachers expect their learners to move beyond shortcuts and memory jingles to understand the meaning behind the mathematics. As in Chapter 2, these teachers differentiate the mathematics tasks by providing varying degrees of complexity and difficulty to their learners. Although every learner will be actively engaged in challenging mathematics tasks that build conceptual understanding of key concepts, Ms. Halstrom, Ms. Fernandez, and Mr. Singh adjust the complexity and difficulty of the task to ensure all learners have access to these concepts.

Ms. Halstrom and Circles and Cylinders

Ms. Halstrom is excited to begin her unit of study about circles. She knows her students enjoy work with manipulatives and visual representations of mathematics and this unit includes both elements. While circles feel like a stand-alone topic, she realizes that they build on ideas of ratio and proportions her students began learning in Grade 6, as well as on area and perimeter students began learning about in Grade 3.

Ms. Halstrom knows some of her students still struggle with computation, especially when fractions or decimals are involved. Because she wants her students to focus on the major concepts in the unit, she plans to make calculators freely available throughout the unit so students can focus their thinking on the big ideas without becoming bogged down in calculations. This means the unit also provides an excellent opportunity for estimation as a check on calculator computation because she knows her students can reason about "a little more than three times as much" when computing with pi. This short unit on circles will also reinforce skills in rounding, as students will see many more decimal places on their calculators than they should record in their work.

What Ms. Halstrom Wants Her Students to Learn

This unit is grounded in a single standard within the second cluster of Grade 7 geometry standards.

MATHEMATICS CONTENT AND PRACTICE STANDARDS

7.G.B

Solve real-life and mathematical problems involving angle measure, area, surface area, and volume.

7.G.B.4

Know the formulas for the area and circumference of a circle and use them to solve problems; give an informal derivation of the relationship between the circumference and area of a circle.

Ms. Halstrom is helping her learners develop the following Standards for Mathematical Practice:

- Reason abstractly and quantitatively.
- Look for and make use of structure.

This opening lesson focuses on the first part of the standard, in particular the formula to compute the circumference of a circle. Although Ms. Halstrom's students have heard of pi, she plans to use this lesson to help them see that pi is actually a ratio, built into the circle itself, rather than the long string of digits some of her students enjoy memorizing for recognition. In this way, the lesson also serves as an application of another standard studied earlier in the year:

MATHEMATICS CONTENT AND PRACTICE STANDARD

7.RP.A.2

Recognize and represent proportional relationships between quantities.

As with every unit Ms. Halstrom teaches, the Standards for Mathematical Practice are as important as the content addressed. While many lessons include multiple practices, she has found that her students focus best when given a lesson that emphasizes only one or two practices. Her students are comfortable with the practices because they are talked about in almost every lesson. Yet Ms. Halstrom is careful to describe what a given practice looks like in each lesson for her students so they have a clear picture of what is expected for success.

Mathematical structure is the idea that any given situation includes parts that are related to one another in a mathematical way. Seeing structure means being able to identify the relevant parts and the relationship between them. When students see pi as a ratio between the circumference and diameter of a circle, they are seeing an underlying structure inherent in all circles. Circles provide a context for a ratio in this case and the activity will ask students to look at measurements for circles in both contextualized and decontextualized ways, in which they see the numbers as values as well as measurements of parts of the circle. This is the key element students will use in the first mathematical practice standard today (reasoning abstractly and quantitatively), realizing that it is easier just to think about the numbers at times (decontextualized values) but that the numbers must always make sense when placed back into context.

This lesson focuses on conceptual understanding. Ms. Halstrom will give her students opportunities to practice calculating the circumference of circles, but that is not today's goal. Today, she wants her students to see the big picture idea that pi is a ratio embedded in the structure of the circle.

Learning Intentions and Success Criteria

Ms. Halstrom knows that students must have clear goals to focus their learning. On this day, her learning intentions focus on both content and language:

Content Learning Intention: I am learning to understand the relationship between circumference and diameter of a circle.

Language Learning Intention: I am learning to use mathematics vocabulary (radius, circumference, diameter, and pi) appropriately when solving problems.

Social Learning Intention: I am learning to engage in productive discussions with my peers about the relationship between the circumference of a circle and the diameter.

The learning intention is deliberately written so that it can be delivered at the beginning of the lesson without serving as a spoiler by revealing the intended "aha" moment. In this lesson, the learning intentions help students focus on the relevant aspects of the learning—they know what they are looking for in their learning. This makes it clear to students that they are looking for a relationship without revealing the nature of the relationship. Ms. Halstrom understands that it is important for students to know the learning intentions for a lesson and that, at times, the learning intention is carefully presented to give students good information about the day's lesson without revealing the mathematics students will eventually discover. The students know that when Ms. Halstrom says "the relationship," there's a puzzle to solve because they have to figure out the relationship. Ms. Halstrom's students enjoy days where the learning intention includes a "secret" because they know there is a puzzle dimension to the day's lesson, and they trust her enough to know that they will have the opportunity to solve the puzzle.

For Ms. Halstrom, these "puzzle days" provide an opportunity to build her students' reasoning and problem-solving skills. She assigns tasks that require students to figure things out rather than her telling them all the key ideas. This works when students have already developed some surface-level knowledge. In this case, students are looking for a relationship, a constant of proportionality (already a familiar idea), in an unexpected

Have a learning intention that contains an element of a "secret" requires high teacher credibility and strong student-teacher relationships.

EFFECT SIZE FOR MOTIVATION = 0.42

EFFECT SIZE FOR TEACHER CREDIBILITY = 0.90 AND TEACHER-STUDENT RELATIONSHIPS = 0.52

place (a circle). They will be measuring and recording the circumference and diameter of a variety of round objects and they will use their data, in a table or graph, to find the constant of proportionality, pi. Knowing this is the focus of learning, Ms. Halstrom identifies several success criteria for her students:

☐ I can accurately and precisely measure the diameter of a circle.

☐ I can build a table of values consistently, using the diameter as the independent variable and the circumference as the dependent variable.

☐ I can find a constant of proportionality between the diameter of a circle and the circumference.

☐ I can interpret the constant of proportionality and explain the significance of this value.

Ms. Halstrom will reveal the first two of these success criteria to the students at the beginning of the lesson when she shares the task. She will be especially watchful that students measure the diameter of the objects across the center of the circle. She also knows that the terms are familiar because both she and her collaborating science teacher use them when talking about variables and relationships. These elements are important to the third success criterion, finding a reasonable approximate value for pi. She will reveal the last two success criteria once students have identified that the relationship between circumference and diameter is proportional.

When she launches this lesson, Ms. Halstrom opens her container of "round things." She has collected bottle caps, yogurt lids, empty jars and cans, paper plates of various sizes, Frisbees, and other circular objects. She even borrows hula hoops from a physical education teacher at her school so students have a very large circle to work with. She divides these materials so each group of students has a variety of objects in a range of sizes. Each group will also need two tape measures. Ms. Halstrom knows from experience to have Wikki Stix™ or some firm twine available for students who struggle with using a tape measure to measure a curved shape. She also knows that stretchy yarn gives distorted results, so she uses twine with as little stretch as possible.

Video 9
Aligning a Conceptual Task to the Learning Intention

https://resources.corwin.com/vlmathematics-6-8

Guiding and Scaffolding Student Thinking

As the students enter the classroom, Ms. Halstrom has placed a collection of round objects and measuring tools at each cluster of four desks. Ms. Halstrom considers her student seating groups at the beginning of each unit of study. Given the lack of evidence for grouping students by perceived ability groups, Ms. Halstrom heterogeneously groups her students such that there is a range of skills around measurement and computation. She has formative evaluation data from exit tickets, student conversations, and problem sets that indicate learners are at different levels of readiness with their measurement and computation skills. She uses a heterogeneous grouping strategy called **alternate group ranking** (Frey, Hattie, & Fisher, 2018). In her class period with 32 students, for example, Ms. Halstrom wants to create groups of four students. To do this, she puts the stack of recent formative evaluation data in descending order from highest score to lowest and starts sorting, one at a time, into eight stacks. This results in the groups shown in Figure 3.1.

These baseline groups are of heterogeneous *current* abilities and provide Ms. Halstrom with an excellent starting point for grouping students. In this case, the highest-achieving students are paired with mid-achieving

Alternate group ranking is based on assessment data and the specific learning needs for specific content.

EFFECT SIZE FOR SMALL GROUP LEARNING = 0.47

ALTERNATE GROUP RANKING

Group 1	Group 2	Group 3	Group 4	Group 5	Group 6	Group 7	Group 8
Student 1	Student 3	Student 5	Student 7	Student 9	Student 11	Student 13	Student 15
Student 2	Student 4	Student 6	Student 8	Student 10	Student 12	Student 14	Student 16
Student 17	Student 19	Student 21	Student 23	Student 25	Student 27	Student 29	Student 31
Student 18	Student 20	Student 22	Student 24	Student 26	Student 28	Student 30	Student 32

Figure 3.1

EFFECT SIZE FOR
ABILITY GROUPING
= 0.12

students and mid-achieving students are paired with lower-achieving students such that the academic diversity in each group is about 50%. She sometimes makes adjustments based on the language needs of her students, specific pairings she knows to be productive, and social concerns (she tries to avoid grouping best friends together, for example). The concept here is that students within a given group are not "too far apart" to communicate productively. Each group is made of two pairs of students whose assessment data are very similar. While there are variations on the specifics of this strategy, younger students tend to benefit from having at least one group member "right next to them" in understanding. Ms. Halstrom considers this a social scaffold. Anecdotally, she also notices that the groups ranked in the middle tend to rise to the leadership roles in most of her classes, as they are close enough in current ability to communicate effectively with all students.

Keeping these new groupings in mind, Ms. Halstrom has designed this day of developing conceptual understanding to be conversational and collaborative. She wants to provide these students opportunities to develop productive working partnerships right out of the gate. As students walk into the classroom during their passing period, Ms. Halstrom has the new groups, along with a new seating chart, displayed on her projector.

EFFECT SIZE FOR
VOCABULARY
INSTRUCTION
= 0.62

The day before this lesson, Ms. Halstrom read *Sir Cumference and the First Round Table* (Neuschwander & Geehan, 1997) to her class. The students learned the definitions of three key vocabulary terms (radius, diameter, and circumference) from this experience. As the class begins, Ms. Halstrom writes the three terms on the board: radius, diameter, and circumference. She asks students to work with the objects in their group and identify the radius, diameter, and circumference of each. She moves around the room listening to the conversation and identifies three groups to model, each addressing a different word, when the class comes back together. She asks one group to model circumference on a round paper plate when she hears a student say, "The circumference is still the very outside edge around, not the distance around here" (pointing to the ridge that defines the lip of the plate). She knows that her students share their thinking more confidently when they have a moment to rehearse within their group. This is particularly true for this class, where a number of students are still building confidence in their spoken English. One

EFFECT SIZE
FOR CLASSROOM
DISCUSSION
= 0.82

group of students is moving back and forth between Arabic and English in their conversation; Ms. Halstrom makes a mental note to circle back to them once the exploration is under way so she can check their English understanding of the vocabulary more closely. She brings the class back together and asks her selected groups to model one term with one of the objects from their table. She says, "I want to make sure you not only know the definition of each term in words but also that you can identify the relevant part on real circular objects." For example, they must recognize that the diameter of a circle is always measured across the middle, even if the object is not perfectly flat as pictured below.

Ms. Halstrom introduces the next tasks by telling the class they will be exploring the circular objects on their tables, measuring both diameter and circumference and then looking for a relationship between these variables. A student quickly asks, "Which variable is independent, Ms. Halstrom?" The teacher smiles, pleased that this vocabulary has settled in well for math and science classes. Ms. Halstrom tells the class that the diameter is the independent variable in this exploration. Circumference will be the dependent variable. She asks each team to create a single data recording sheet for their team.

Teaching Takeaway

Conceptual understanding can be at the surface, deep, or transfer phase of learning.

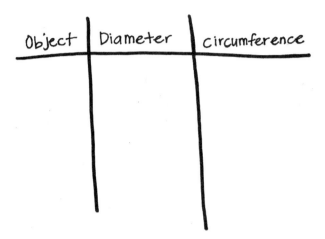

After she reminds students that they should take turns and check each other's work, as always, Ms. Halstrom releases the students to start measuring and adding data to their chart while she returns to check vocabulary with the one group who concerned her at the beginning of class.

Instructional Approaches That Promote Conceptual Understanding

As the students work, Ms. Halstrom circulates around the room. At her first stop, she asks the students who concerned her earlier to show her the radius, diameter, and circumference of the objects at their table. When they can show her these parts of circular objects correctly, she moves on to listen to other groups. Ms. Halstrom notices as she moves around the room that some groups are measuring in inches and using fractions, while other groups are using centimeter measurements and decimals. After confirming that each group is using the same units for all measures on their table, Ms. Halstrom decides not to say anything about these different group decisions. It would not impact the outcome of the work, even when measurements were pulled together, and it would provide an interesting point for conversation, adding complexity to the lesson.

As Ms. Halstrom listens to students, she notices correct vocabulary and observes for appropriate measurement techniques and accurate measurements. When she sees a student struggle because the tape measure isn't long enough to go around the hula hoop, she hands him some firm twine so he can make a string the length of the circumference and then measure that. At another group, the twine is useful for measuring the diameter of a bottle cap that is almost completely covered by the tape measure. As students progress through the activity, Ms. Halstrom encourages them to describe the relationship they see between the independent and dependent variables when talking with their group. "I think I can predict the circumference of the next object," Abeer says as her partner measures the diameter of a Frisbee. "Each circumference is a little bigger than three times the diameter. If this diameter is 24 centimeters, the circumference will be around 75 centimeters." Michael measures the circumference as 76.5 centimeters. "Close enough," he comments. "What kind of relationship do you see here?" Ms. Halstrom asks. When Abeer responds that this looks like a proportion, Ms. Halstrom encourages the group to add a fourth column to their data chart and to calculate values for that column, the ratio between circumference and diameter; this purposeful question is designed to get them thinking about their findings. As groups finish collecting data for their objects, Ms. Halstrom asks them to use a calculator or computer to find the ratio of circumference to diameter for each object and an overall constant of proportionality. When one group asks if they should make a graph of their data, Ms. Halstrom encourages this additional representation. Conversation in the room grows louder as students realize their values look like that familiar number, π.

Object	Diameter (cm)	Circumference (cm)	Ratio C:D
1	22.2	69.8	3.14
2	4	13.3	3.325
3	5.5	17.6	3.2
4	3.7	13.2	3.57
5	15.8	49.6	3.14

Teaching for Clarity at the Close

Ms. Halstrom brings the class together and reveals the third and fourth success criteria for the lesson. After she reads the third criterion, she asks several groups to share their ratios or constants of proportionality. When she asks groups to share how they determined the constant of proportionality, she carefully sequences the process (Smith & Stein, 2011). The first group to share made an estimate by looking at the ratio column and the second group calculated an average ratio. The third group to share has created a graph of their data to find the point (1, r), transferring their learning from an earlier lesson about unit rate. The students identify the point (1, 3.2) and note that 3.2 is their unit rate for the graph even though they have no object with a diameter of 1. This is an excellent transfer of their learning from the earlier unit on proportional relationships. Ms. Halstrom points to the fourth success criterion for the lesson (interpreting the constant of proportionality) and asks students what it means that the constant of proportionality is pi. One student responds, "It means that if you multiply the diameter by pi, you can find the circumference of the circle." Ms. Halstrom encourages the students to reflect for a moment and talk with their partners about whether they agree with this statement.

EFFECT SIZE FOR TRANSFER STRATEGIES = 0.86

EFFECT SIZE FOR EVALUATION AND REFLECTION = 0.75

Because Ms. Halstrom knows the science teacher has been discussing error in his class, she asks the class why the ratio was not 3.14 for every circle measured. Partners talk quietly and Ms. Halstrom asks one student for her explanation. The student describes the challenge her group had keeping their tape measure flat against the edge of some objects and tells the class this means their measurement is a little bit off. Ms. Halstrom states, "That's error, the mistakes you make even though you are trying your best. No one is perfect." Ms. Halstrom pauses as she sees some groups re-measure an object where their ratio was particularly different from 3.14. There are smiles of pleasure as measurements are refined and ratios are more accurately calculated. This tells Ms. Halstrom that students understand the concept and see that the underlying relationship is true even if their measurements do not precisely reflect the relationship.

EFFECT SIZE FOR MASTERY LEARNING = 0.57

At this point, the success criteria for the lesson have been met. There is some additional time, so Ms. Halstrom considers her options. One

possibility is to foreshadow the upcoming unit on statistics and probability by looking at the class data pooled together. The second option
is to begin to connect the conceptual understanding established today
to the procedural fluency required to use the formula correctly. Given
that the statistics and probability unit is still far in the future, she
decides to save the data from each group to use then and moves ahead
to finding the formula.

Ms. Halstrom asks the class to remind her (and each other) of all the
different ways they know to represent ratios or proportional relationships. The class quickly lists the graphs and tables they have used today.
One student gives a verbal description, "The circumference of a circle is
a little more than three times the length of the diameter," and another
student notices that it sounds like an equation. Ms. Halstrom asks her
to explain. "If I said it like this: 'The circumference is pi times the diameter of the circle,' that could be written like this." The student writes
$C = \pi d$ on the whiteboard at her table and holds it up for the class to
see. Ms. Halstrom decides to end the class with a question: she writes
$\frac{c}{d} = \pi \approx 3.14$ on the board and reminds the class that this is the way they
have learned to write equations for ratios. She asks the students to think
about how these two equations are related to each other and tells them
the discussion will continue the next day. Students write the equations
in their notebooks and straighten their materials before leaving the
classroom at the bell.

With a planning period in the second hour, Ms. Halstrom has time to
reflect on this first implementation of the lesson and refine it for classes
later in the day. As she reflects, she notices several good things about
her lesson.

1. Her students were using multiple representations of the mathematics and making connections without prompting from the
   teacher. In all groups, students were connecting the dimensions
   of the objects to the values in the table, connecting the physical
   with the symbolic. In the group who made a graph, they connected this visual representation to the other two.

2. Her students were comfortable with the measuring tools.
   Ms. Halstrom had heard this from her science teacher colleague

but was glad to see it herself. Knowing that her students like a challenge, she decided to pull out some golf balls and Ping-Pong balls from her collection. She could add one of these spheres to the tables of students who were moving quickly through the measurement task to provide a higher level of difficulty where students were ready.

3. It surprised her to finish the lesson with some time remaining in class. While she was pleased with her connection to the procedural lesson planned for the next day, Ms. Halstrom decided she would prefer to push students on representing their proportional relationships graphically if she had the additional time in later classes. She decided to revise her instructions to require both a table and a graph from each group. Knowing that different students preferred different tools (a graphing calculator, a spreadsheet, or graphing software), she decided to continue allowing each group to choose their graphing tool. This would mean more work to pool the data later, but that was a fair trade to build confidence in graphing skills.

4. In terms of student learning, Ms. Halstrom was very pleased. Even some of her students who were still struggling with proportional relationships could explain the relationship they saw in the circular objects and recognize the value as pi. A quick glance at her daily log showed that she had heard from every student in the class at some point, in either table conversation or sharing with the whole class. As she reviewed the data tables from each group, she saw appropriate measurements and calculations, supporting her observations of student learning. She was confident the students understood the mathematics from today's lesson and was looking forward to making new connections tomorrow.

Figure 3.2 shows how Ms. Halstrom made her planning visible so that she could then provide an engaging and rigorous learning experience for her learners.

Ms. Halstrom's Teaching for Clarity PLANNING GUIDE

ESTABLISHING PURPOSE

1 What are the key content standards I will focus on in this lesson?

Content Standards:

7.G.B

Solve real-life and mathematical problems involving angle measure, area, surface area, and volume.

7.G.B.4

Know the formulas for the area and circumference of a circle and use them to solve problems; give an informal derivation of the relationship between the circumference and area of a circle.

Standards for Mathematical Practice:

- Reason abstractly and quantitatively.
- Look for and make use of structure.

2 What are the learning intentions (the goal and *why* of learning, stated in student-friendly language) I will focus on in this lesson?

Content: I am learning to understand the relationship between circumference and diameter of a circle.

Language: I am learning to use mathematics vocabulary (radius, circumference, diameter, and pi) appropriately when solving problems.

Social: I am learning to engage in productive discussions with my peers about the relationship between the circumference of a circle and the diameter.

3 When will I introduce and reinforce the learning intention(s) so that students understand it, see the relevance, connect it to previous learning, and can clearly communicate it themselves?

I will discuss the learning intentions at the beginning of class, emphasizing that students are looking to identify the type of relationship they see between diameter and circumference of a circle. We will also discuss the first two success criteria at the beginning of class. I will hold the final two success criteria for discussion until after students have identified the relationship as proportional.

SUCCESS CRITERIA

4 What evidence shows that students have mastered the learning intention(s)? What criteria will I use?

I can statements:

- I can accurately and precisely measure the diameter of a circle (*Note to self: watch out that students measure across the center point).
- I can build a table of values consistently, using the diameter as the independent variable and the circumference as the dependent variable.
- I can find a constant of proportionality between the diameter of a circle and the circumference.
- I can interpret the constant of proportionality and explain the significance of this value.

5 How will I check students' understanding (assess learning) during instruction and make accommodations?

As learners engage in the task, I will first observe for careful and accurate measurements. As students gather data, I will ask them to describe the pattern they see in the graph or table of values for their measurements. I will also ask students to estimate circumference given diameter (or vice versa), looking for a ratio of about 3 or a little more than 3.

INSTRUCTION

6 **What activities and tasks will move students forward in their learning?**

Students will work in small groups to collect and organize measurements of round objects-how far across and how far around.

They will use their knowledge of proportionality to search for a constant of proportionality using tables and graphs.

As a whole class, we will pool data into a class data set and refine the value of pi.

7 **What resources (materials and sentence frames) are needed?**

1. Measuring tapes

2. Wikki Stix or firm twine (optional; not yarn, because it stretches too much)

3. Round objects-large collection in varying sizes from bottle caps to hula hoops (yogurt or whipped topping lids, Frisbees, cans or bottles, plates in varying sizes, etc.)

4. Grid paper for making a table of data and graph

8 **How will I organize and facilitate the learning? What questions will I ask? How will I initiate closure?**

1. Lesson Introduction

- The lesson opens with each group applying the vocabulary from yesterday's book reading (diameter, circumference, and radius) to objects on their table. Each student team will have an assigned group of objects and measurement tools. After this brief review, present the learning intentions and first two success criteria for the task.

2. Student Activity

- Students measure their assigned objects and record the measurements while looking for patterns. I will circulate during this time. Students will organize their data into tables and graphs, working either by hand or by computer as the group prefers. Groups will be organized so that there are a range of skills (e.g., a good organizer, a good grapher, and a good measurer) on the team.

3. Lesson Closure

- After students recognize the common unit rate of pi, I will share the third and fourth success criteria, which will lead to a discussion of the meaning of the constant of proportionality.

online resources ▸ This lesson plan is available for download at resources.corwin.com/vlmathematics-6-8.

Figure 3.2 Ms. Halstrom's Conceptual Understanding Lesson on Circles and Cylinders

Ms. Fernandez and Systems of Linear Equations

EFFECT SIZE FOR PRIOR ABILITY = 0.94

EFFECT SIZE FOR STRATEGY TO INTEGRATE WITH PRIOR KNOWLEDGE = 0.93

In a previous unit, students in Ms. Fernandez's eighth grade class dove deep into linear functions. They calculated rates of change and predicted points (including x- and y-intercepts) from given values, graphed lines, and mathematically modeled real-world scenarios with linear functions. As she begins this next unit on systems of equations, Ms. Fernandez intends to leverage her students' understanding of graphing to help them understand what a system of equations is and what the solution to a system might look like. Her students have developed proficiency at interpreting graphs of single linear functions, including extracting explicit functions from simple graphs by locating the y-intercept and identifying the slope. Therefore, Ms. Fernandez decides she will start this day of conceptual understanding there.

What Ms. Fernandez Wants Her Students to Learn

Ms. Fernandez wants to dedicate the bulk of this class period to the *concept* of a system of equations and its solution so that she can later build procedural fluency that is grounded and has meaning for students. Essentially, by building a new conceptual understanding *today*, she is sowing the seeds and building the need for additional procedural knowledge *tomorrow*. This is why she will be focusing on the single standard listed below.

MATHEMATICS CONTENT AND PRACTICE STANDARDS

8.EE.C.8

Analyze and solve pairs of simultaneous linear equations.

a. Understand that solutions to a system of two linear equations in two variables correspond to points of intersection of their graphs, because points of intersection satisfy both equations simultaneously.

Ms. Fernandez is helping her learners develop the following Standards for Mathematical Practice:

- Reason abstractly and quantitatively.
- Look for and make use of structure.

Conceptual understanding is at the heart of this standard. Notice that the key verb in this standard (and first word) is *understand*. The verb *understand* is a challenging one in the standards because it appears often and has a variety of meanings. In this context, the focus of understanding is on making sense of the graphical representation of the solution (Usiskin, 2012).

Teaching Takeaway

We must be clear on the expectations articulated in the content standards and standards for mathematical practice or process to ensure teaching and learning are aligned with the standard.

Learning Intentions and Success Criteria

As mentioned in the previous chapter, Ms. Fernandez utilizes the *content*, *language*, and *social* varieties of learning intentions so that she can focus on specific areas of growth for each category. Her learning intentions for this lesson are as follows:

> *Content Learning Intention:* I am learning to understand that the intersection of two lines on a graph represents the solution to two simultaneous linear equations.
>
> *Language Learning Intention:* I am learning to articulate the meaning of solutions of systems of equations both abstractly and within a specific context.
>
> *Social Learning Intention:* I am learning to communicate our thinking to our peers even before we completely understand a topic.

Ms. Fernandez begins her day by introducing these learning intentions and using their language as a means of communicating her expectations:

> Today is about using the tools we already have to think about something new. It's a new unit. We haven't talked about these things before. But don't let that stop you from thinking out loud with your partners. This is why our social learning intention today is to communicate our thinking to our peers even before we completely understand a topic. Remember, you deserve to know this stuff—so let's talk it out.

EFFECT SIZE FOR SELF-EFFICACY = 0.92

She finishes her introduction by asking the students to turn to their neighbors and say, "We got this!" Ms. Fernandez models this can-do attitude and behavior by showing her passion for the subject and for her own students' learning. She knows that student-teacher relationships have a considerable impact on students' learning and she uses these displays of advocacy to further those relationships. Students are more likely to take risks for teachers they trust.

EFFECT SIZE FOR STUDENT-TEACHER RELATIONSHIPS = 0.52

EFFECT SIZE FOR TEACHER CREDIBILITY = 0.90

Ms. Fernandez is laser focused on the intent that students understand the meaning of a graphical representation as a means of measuring what conceptual understanding looks like in this context. This is why the success criteria for the lesson emphasize the appearance of the graph and making sense of the elements of the graph. Rather than simply rewriting the standard with the words "I can" in front of it, Ms. Fernandez put a great deal of thought into what it means for students to be able to understand that the intersection of two lines on a graph *represents* the solution to two simultaneous linear equations. She asked herself what progress along the path to mastering this standard looks like for her learners. What underlying mathematics is required in service of this standard? What are some mile markers that indicate partial progress toward mastery? Although this particular standard (8a) focuses on the mathematics of graphing systems, Ms. Fernandez knows that her students are stronger when they look at mathematics through a contextual lens. In addition, other parts of the standard (particularly 8c) include contextual representations, so she decides to include elements of meaning in today's success criteria. Ultimately, she breaks them down into three categories:

> ☐ I can describe a graph as a set of points that satisfies an equation and identify the meaning of a given point on the graph.
>
> ☐ I can explain how the intersection of two lines represents a point where both equations are true.
>
> ☐ I can explain the meaning of a solution to a system of equations mathematically and within a context.

The first criterion addresses some prior knowledge that her students will bring to bear when mastering this standard: they need to be able to describe a graph of a linear function if they are going to find and explain solutions to linear systems on a graph. The second criterion gets to the heart of the standard. Students must recognize that the point of intersection makes both equations true and begin to interpret the mathematical implications of that fact. The final criterion gets at the interpretation of a solution—both abstractly and in the concrete. Ms. Fernandez unpacked the standard's expectation of representational understanding into three subparts: describe the

Teaching Takeaway

Success criteria should provide a clear path toward mastery of the learning intention.

Teaching Takeaway

Conceptual understanding can be at the deep phase of learning. This occurs when learners are making connections between concepts.

EFFECT SIZE FOR COGNITIVE TASK ANALYSIS = 1.29

representation, explain the key point on the graph, and make meaning of the result.

Breaking success criteria down in this fashion also allows students to identify specifically where their learning might be stalling. For example, maybe students are able to describe a graph but cannot explain the meaning of a given point. These formative data should elicit a different response from the teacher (and student), rather than the other way around. This method also gives teachers a natural response to the vague "I don't get it" types of responses. Ms. Fernandez likes to respond simply with "What don't you get?" as she prompts students to refer to their *I can* statements. She will continue, "Can you . . . ?" as she reads off each success criterion. Admittedly, students may find this frustrating if they are new to this type of classroom culture. Many students arrive trained to simply seek out the "right answers" and the "right way to do problems." Building an expectation of metacognition, self-assessment, and critical thinking can be a challenging culture shock for these students. Ms. Fernandez feels an obligation to further her students down their own paths to becoming assessment-capable visible learners.

To support her students in their progress toward being assessment-capable mathematics learners, Ms. Fernandez asks them to engage in a think-pair-share with today's success criteria. She asks, "As you look over today's criteria for success, which of these do you have prior knowledge about and which ones generate questions in your mind?" After she pauses for a minute, she asks her learners to turn to a neighbor and talk through what they already know about the day's success criteria and where they have questions. Ms. Fernandez listens to the students as she moves around the room, and she makes note of specific patterns in their conversations. For example, she writes in the margin of her lesson plan that each pair or trio of learners is discussing the process for creating graphs but they say they struggle with identifying the meaning of specific points on the graph. None of her learners are talking about the meaning of solutions. One student says, "I have no idea what the last one [success criterion] is talking about." The partner quickly responds, "Maybe that's what we're going to do today." These conversations provide valuable data and evidence that Ms. Fernandez has identified the right level of challenge.

Ms. Fernandez says, "Alright folks, please pause your conversations. After listening in on your conversations, I was very excited to hear you talk about how you construct graphs and find solutions to equations."

A student chimes in, "Yeah, but what about the meaning. I don't know what you mean by meaning."

Ms. Fernandez takes this opportunity to transition to the day's learning, saying, "That is exactly what we are going to learn today."

Instructional Approaches That Promote Conceptual Understanding

Ms. Fernandez is truly hybridizing dialogic and deliberate instructional approaches in this lesson by engaging in a back-and-forth with students. She plans to prompt students to discuss a series of questions using the think-pair-share protocol, whereby students first take time to individually think about their responses before discussing with a partner and ultimately sharing their collaborative thinking with another group. Her goal with this dialogic approach is to allow students the opportunity to activate their prior knowledge, experience the perturbation required for new learning to occur, and begin to construct their own understanding of the concept.

Of course, Ms. Fernandez listens to their conversations, noting any errors so that she can plan subsequent instruction based on misconceptions. To address the issues she has identified, she models her own thinking through a think-aloud. This direct approach gives students the ability to witness how an expert would approach a given situation or problem. Ms. Fernandez recognizes that the effect sizes for both dialogic instruction and direct/deliberate instruction are above the hinge point and that she doesn't need to choose *which* to use exclusively, but *when* to use each (and for what purpose).

EFFECT SIZE FOR DIALOGIC INSTRUCTION = 0.82 AND DIRECT/ DELIBERATE INSTRUCTION = 0.60

Teaching Takeaway

Using the right approach at the right time increases our impact on student learning in the mathematics classroom.

GRAPHED SYSTEM OF EQUATIONS IN A CONTEXT: THE NUMBER OF NICKELS AND DIMES IN A JAR

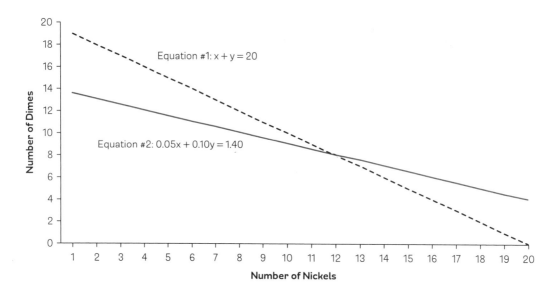

Figure 3.3

Ms. Fernandez engages her students in another think-pair-share by prompting them to look at a projected image of a graphed system of equations in a context (Figure 3.3).

The context is not explicitly spelled out for students, but the graph is labeled so that inferences may be drawn. For example, the y-axis is labeled "number of dimes" and the x-axis "number of nickels." Without describing the image herself, Ms. Fernandez begins with "Take a moment and think about the following question by yourself. No talking for this first part. . . . What are the key features of the dashed line this graph that will help communicate its meaning?" She repeats the question a second time as she notes her students' expressions while they look at the image and hear the question. After about 20 seconds of independent think time, Ms. Fernandez instructs her students, "Okay, now turn to your partner and discuss your responses to the question."

While her students are buzzing with conversation, Ms. Fernandez notes the engagement level of each pair. She is working to anticipate who will need more support, be it academically, socially, or linguistically. She checks in with one pair that has ceased conversing and seems to be avoiding eye contact. "Hi team," she begins. "What did we talk about here? What are the key features of the dashed line on this graph that will help communicate its meaning?" One student laughs nervously while the other shrugs. Ms. Fernandez tries again. "What does the y-axis tell us? What does it say?"

One of the students responds, "The number of dimes."

"Number of dimes? What does that mean, having a certain number of dimes tells you what?" Ms. Fernandez questions.

"The amount of money, you know, like 30 cents," the other student responds.

"The amount of money?" she asks. "How do you know?"

The first student sits up in his chair and leans into the conversation, pointing at the projected image. He says, "There are two equations that tell me how many dimes and nickels I have. It says it right there! But why do I need two equations to tell me this?" Ms. Fernandez looks at the other student who nods in agreement.

Seizing this opportunity to develop self-efficacy, Ms. Fernandez concludes this check-in with "Awesome, thank you both. What you're doing right now is identifying the meaning of points on a graph. That's part of your first *I can* statement. Please see what else you can figure out about the graph, like why you have two equations, as I check in with other tables."

Ms. Fernandez continues her scan briefly before bringing her students' attention back to the front of the class: "Welcome back, class. Who would like to share what your pair talked about? What does the dashed line on this graph tell us? How are you making sense of it?"

After taking a handful of responses and allowing students to openly converse and build off of each other, Ms. Fernandez repeats this process with the following, preplanned focusing questions, all designed to build toward the first criterion for success:

- Which equation is represented by the dashed line on the graph: $y = 20 - x$ or $y = 14 - 0.5x$?

- What does this tell us about the meaning of a given point on the line?

> **EFFECT SIZE FOR FEEDBACK = 0.70**

> **Teaching Takeaway**
>
> Our feedback to learners must be specific and constructive so that learners can assimilate the feedback into their thinking.

Teaching Takeaway

During our planning time, we must consider carefully the types of questions we will ask our students and when we will ask them. This cannot always be done in the moment.

- Describe the situation represented by the red line. What key features made you describe it in that way?

- What are the key features of this graph that help communicate its meaning?

Moving toward the second success criterion, Ms. Fernandez presents the following scenario to her students, which is associated with the two equations presented in the graph:

Ms. Fernandez has a jar of nickels and dimes on her desk. If you can identify the correct number of nickels and dimes, you get the money in the jar to spend at the concession stand during field day. Here are two pieces of information about the contents of the jar: (1) there are 20 coins in the jar; (2) the total value of the jar is $1.40.

She now asks the students to revisit the previous questions in light of this scenario. She adds two additional questions for consideration:

- What does this point of intersection represent mathematically? What does the intersection mean in the context?

- In the context, what was happening before the intersection and what happens after the intersection?

Some questions require longer think times and longer pair discussions than others and Ms. Fernandez is comfortable providing that time. She tries to gauge the quality of the students' conversations to determine when to move on. After all, this is *their* time that she has set aside to develop a conceptual understanding.

Modeling Strategies and Skills

After completing each set of questions, Ms. Fernandez switches from the dialogic think-pair-share strategy to the deliberate strategy of expert modeling via a think-aloud. She projects another labeled graph and requests that her students listen carefully while she models her thinking for them (Figure 3.4).

GRAPHED SYSTEM OF EQUATIONS IN A CONTEXT: THE COST OF GOING TO THE MOVIES

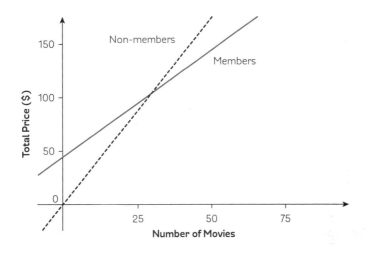

Figure 3.4

Ms. Fernandez says, "Here is another pair of graphs for us to consider. This time I want you to listen to my thinking about the graphs and the meaning of the intersection. As you listen, think about how my explanation and thinking can extend your own thinking." Once she sets up the expectations of the think-aloud, she begins as follows:

> When I see this graph, the first thing that I notice is that the y-axis is labeled "total price in dollars" and the x-axis is labeled "number of movies." This tells me that I am looking at the amount of money you spend to watch a certain number of movies. I am also recognizing that my x-axis is counting movies in increments of 5. My y-axis is counting the total cost in increments of $10. Does everybody agree with this description of the graph, so far? Turn to your partner and tell that person why you agree or disagree.

Ms. Fernandez pauses and allows students to talk. She notes that they are thinking along with her and that they can defend their responses.

She continues, "Now as I investigate these two lines further, I notice something interesting. Look at the *y*-intercepts. For this dotted line, if I don't go to any movies, I don't spend any money. For the red line, it looks like I spend $45 even if I don't go to any movies. " Ms. Fernandez explicitly gestures to the part of the graph that she is interpreting as she describes it. "What could that be about? Let's look at some other points on each line. Here on the dotted line, when I've been to 15 movies, I've spend $50. On the solid line, when I've been to 15 movies, I've spent about $75. Choose another number of movies and see how much each line shows you would spend." Ms. Fernandez pauses for her students to talk. She hears good interpretations of the points on the lines in the graph, so she continues.

> I also see that the two lines are labeled—members and non-members. I wondered what that means so I read about this graph a little bit. On this graph, the solid line represents people who are members of the movie club. They pay an annual membership fee and then the price of each movie ticket is lower. Non-members don't pay that fee but their price for each ticket is higher. The membership fee is $45, the money members have spent before they go to a movie. Does everybody agree with my claim? Are there any clarifying questions about how I've said this?

After she allows questions from her students, Ms. Fernandez continues her think-aloud.

EFFECT SIZE FOR
SUMMARIZATION
= 0.79

> When you chose a number of movies to discuss earlier, did anyone select 30 movies? How much does it cost to attend 30 movies? I'm interested in this point because it's where the two lines intersect. That means that for 30 movies, you pay the same amount of money, $105, whether you're part of the club or not. Notice that the coordinates for the intersecting point are (30, 105). Turn to your partners and tell them what makes the most sense about how I thought through this problem and what makes the least sense about my process.

Explicit teacher modeling is a difficult skill for many math teachers to build. As math students ourselves, we are often trained to become more efficient and begin pruning what we feel are unnecessary steps and computational deadweight. The trouble with this path to efficiency is that these trimmings become expert blind spots when we run a classroom of our own. Many of us have lived through educational experiences where we were taught to *seek the right answers as quickly as possible*. With a core shift to viewing mathematics as a *process* rather than a collection of *products*, it is important for us as educators to investigate our own problem-solving processes and regrow any trimmed blind spots. It helps to think about mathematics itself as an explanation, where each individual step comes with purpose and justifiable legitimacy.

Ms. Fernandez provides her students three additional graphs of systems to interpret. She distributes the first graph to all of the students (Figure 3.5) and then provides the following graphs as students can explain the first graph to her. The graphs become increasingly complex, allowing the work on the task to be differentiated as student pairs progress at their own rate. At the end of the lesson, Ms. Fernandez provides time to work on a collaborative task aligned to the day's success criteria.

For this new task, students are presented a graph representing two mobile phone plans. This is a familiar context because they've worked with this in earlier units about linear functions. They must respond in writing to the following prompt:

> What amount of cell phone usage makes Monthly Plan #1 less expensive? What amount of usage makes Monthly Plan #2 less expensive? Explain your reasoning using the values of each graph at specific points on the graphs. Make sure that the point of intersection is one of the points you use in your explanation.

Students turn this written task in at the end of the day so that Ms. Fernandez may use the data formatively to provide feedback and plan the following day of learning.

Teaching Takeaway

Exit tickets are a way to formatively evaluate learning in our mathematics classroom. Student responses on exit tickets provide data on where to go next.

GRAPHED SYSTEM OF EQUATIONS IN A CONTEXT: THE COST OF TWO MOBILE PHONE PLANS

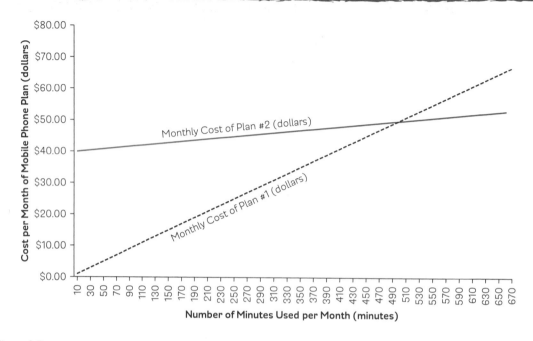

Figure 3.5

Teaching for Clarity at the Close

Ms. Fernandez ends this day of conceptual understanding with a brief whole-class share-out. She asks students to journal each of the following questions in their notebooks before discussing each as a class:

- Explain what is meant by the "solution" of a system of equations.
- How does this relate to their graphs?

She ends by asking her students to take a minute to re-read through their *I can* statements and check the boxes that they are feeling confident about. Figure 3.6 shows how Ms. Fernandez made her planning visible so that she could then provide an engaging and rigorous learning experience for her learners.

Ms. Fernandez's Teaching for Clarity PLANNING GUIDE

ESTABLISHING PURPOSE

1

What are the key content standards I will focus on in this lesson?

Content Standards:

8.EE.C.8

Analyze and solve pairs of simultaneous linear equations.

a. Understand that solutions to a system of two linear equations in two variables correspond to points of intersection of their graphs, because points of intersection satisfy both equations simultaneously.

Standards for Mathematical Practice:

- Reason abstractly and quantitatively.
- Look for and make use of structure.

2

What are the learning intentions (the goal and why of learning, stated in student-friendly language) I will focus on in this lesson?

Content: I am learning to understand that the intersection of two lines on a graph represents the solution to two simultaneous linear equations.

Language: I am learning to articulate the meaning of solutions of systems of equations both abstractly and within a specific context.

Social: I am learning to communicate our thinking to our peers even before we completely understand a topic.

3

When will I introduce and reinforce the learning intention(s) so that students understand it, see the relevance, connect it to previous learning, and can clearly communicate it themselves?

I will open the day with an explanation of the learning intentions and brief expansion of each. I really want to emphasize the social intention today so that students can practice thinking out loud as they problem solve. Transparent struggle is important for collaboration. I will also reiterate the language intention as we discuss and explain points on our graph.

SUCCESS CRITERIA

4

What evidence shows that students have mastered the learning intention(s)? What criteria will I use?

I can statements:

- *I can describe a graph as a set of points which satisfies an equation and identify the meaning of a given point on the graph.*
- *I can explain how the intersection of two lines represents a point where both equations are true.*
- *I can explain the meaning of a solution to a system of equations mathematically and within a context.*

5

How will I check students' understanding (assess learning) during instruction and make accommodations?

During direct instruction, I will be using the think-pair-share protocol so students can process the concepts with a peer and I can formatively assess their conversations and responses. This will also give me the chance to note who will need additional guided practice when we transition to collaborative work time. Finally, today's task comprehensively addresses and assesses each success criterion. I will collect the task at the end of the day and use these data to create tomorrow's study-group stations.

INSTRUCTION

6 **What activities and tasks will move students forward in their learning?**

1. *Think-Pair-Share/Direct Instruction Combo*

   I will ask students to process questions in think-pair-share format and I will model specific skills and strategies based on their responses/needs. I want to give them the chance to make discoveries and teach each other first.

2. *Collaborative Task: Analyzing Systems*

   This task is designed to help students show their understanding of the meaning of the point of intersection on the graph of a system.

7 **What resources (materials and sentence frames) are needed?**

1. *Printed copies of each graph for student pairs*
2. *Printed copies of the task for each learner*

8 **How will I organize and facilitate the learning? What questions will I ask? How will I initiate closure?**

1. *Think-Pair-Share*

   a. *Organize students into pairs and instruct the learning intentions of the day. Have students record success criteria in their notebooks.*

   b. *Project an image of a graph of a system in a context. Which equation is represented by each line on the graph (provide two choices)? What does this tell us about the meaning of a given point on the line? Describe the situation represented by each line. What key features made you describe it in that way? What are the key features of this graph that help communicate its meaning? What does this point of intersection represent mathematically? What does the intersection mean in the context? In the context, what was happening before the intersection and what happens after the intersection?*

c. Project another image of a graph of a system in a different context. Model the sense-making process by answering the preceding questions again in a think-aloud. Explicitly link my think-aloud to Success Criteria 1, 2, and 3 when I model that behavior.

2. Pair Work: Analyzing Systems Task

Students work in their pairs to answer questions on the final task. These questions are aligned to the second and third success criteria for the lesson.

3. Closure: Share-Out

a. Explain what is meant by the "solution" of a system of equations.

b. How does this relate to their graphs?

c. How does this relate to tables of values?

d. Take a minute and re-read through your I can statements and check the boxes that you are feeling confident about.

online resources — This lesson plan is available for download at resources.corwin.com/vlmathematics-6-8.

Figure 3.6   Ms. Fernandez's Conceptual Understanding Lesson on Systems of Linear Equations

Mr. Singh and Integers

Mr. Singh's sixth graders are excited. They are going to start learning about negative numbers today as the unit on integers begins. He has planned the unit to build off the intuitive understanding of integers his students are beginning to develop. Officially, this is the first time students are studying integers. In reality, he knows that students have been exposed to the concept in real life as well as in other mathematics classes. They are familiar with contexts like losing yardage in a game and borrowing money; these will serve as Mr. Singh's entry point for the unit.

What Mr. Singh Wants His Students to Learn

Mr. Singh's standards address a range of topics about integers. Students must first understand integers, including comparing and ordering them along with the concept of absolute value. In addition, students will learn about operations with integers, expanding from their knowledge of operations with whole numbers, fractions, and decimals. In this first lesson of the unit, Mr. Singh wants to make students aware of what they already know about integers and help them learn the vocabulary, notation, and representations they will use as they learn about integers.

> ## Teaching Takeaway
>
> Teaching mathematics in the Visible Learning classroom is possible regardless of your state's specific standards. Standards tell us what to teach, not how.

MATHEMATICS CONTENT AND PRACTICE STANDARDS

Virginia Standards of Learning 6.6

The student will

a. add, subtract, multiply, and divide integers;

b. solve practical problems involving operations with integers; and

c. simplify numerical expressions involving integers.

Mr. Singh is helping his learners develop the following Virginia Mathematical Process Goal for Students:

• Mathematical representations

Learning Intentions and Success Criteria

Within these broad standards, Mr. Singh has identified specific learning intentions for this lesson. He wants to be certain his students understand what they are learning and what is expected of them in this lesson. The focus of today's lesson is on using the language and representations of integers to describe situations already familiar to students.

Teaching Takeaway

Learning intentions should incorporate the Standards for Mathematical Practice or process standards.

Content Learning Intention: I am learning to understand that real-world situations require positive and negative numbers.

Language Learning Intention: I am learning to use words (*positive, negative, opposite, sign*) and symbols (+, –) correctly when speaking and writing about positive and negative numbers.

Social Learning Intention: I am learning to work collaboratively with my partner to complete today's task.

It is not only important to establish goals to focus learning in the class but also essential for students (and the teacher) to know what success looks like in the lesson. In this case, Mr. Singh is looking for students to correctly identify situations as reflecting positive or negative numbers. He also wants them to correctly represent the values of a given situation using a number line and/or two-color counters. Thus, the success criteria for today represent a learning progression related to integers.

- ☐ I can correctly identify situations involving positive and/or negative numbers.
- ☐ I can represent the integers in a given problem on a number line.
- ☐ I can represent the values of a given situation using two-color counters.
- ☐ I can compare the values of positive and negative numbers.

Teaching Takeaway

Surface learning focuses on single representations. Learners will deepen their learning when they begin to make connections between these representations.

In this initial lesson, Mr. Singh is focused on students using each representation correctly more than on making connections between representations; that will come in later in their learning.

Guiding and Scaffolding Student Thinking

At the beginning of class, Mr. Singh asks his students to get out their individual dry erase boards, along with markers and erasers. The class routinely shares their thinking by using the boards; they are a valuable tool for Mr. Singh because he is able to quickly see what each individual student is thinking. He says, "Sketch an open number line on your board. I'll describe a situation and you represent the value on the number line. Let's try an example. You are given $10 in birthday money." The students sketch quickly and hold up their boards. Mr. Singh is not surprised when all represent +10 correctly. He quickly sketches a number line marked at +10 on the board and labels it *birthday money*. "Okay, erase that one and let's do another one. You score six points in the game." Again, students represent +6 correctly and Mr. Singh sketches on the board. He asks, "Ready for something different? Erase the score from the game. Now think about this. You borrow $5 from dad to go to the movies on the weekend." There's a pause in the class while students think about what to sketch. The students hold up their sketches and Mr. Singh asks two students to come to the front of the room. They hold their graphs up for the class to see and Mr. Singh asks them to explain their graphs (Figure 3.7).

EFFECT SIZE FOR INDUCTIVE TEACHING = 0.44

The first student (A) explains his graph by saying this is $5 just like the birthday money is $10. The second student (B) explains hers by saying

GRAPHED INTEGER VALUES IN A CONTEXT: MOVIE MONEY

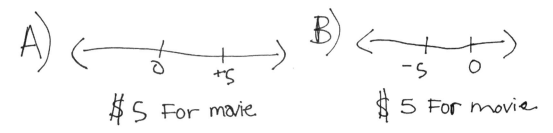

Figure 3.7

that it is money but this time you owe the money instead of having the money so it belongs on the other side. As is typical in this classroom, Mr. Singh asks the class to turn to a shoulder partner and talk about how they thought about the situation and which sketch they agree with. The class understands that learning is more important than getting the right answer on the first go, especially with a new concept. As he listens, Mr. Singh hears and sees several students who graphed +5 change their thinking to –5 as they consider the idea of opposites. Next, students share their thinking with the whole class, coming to a tentative consensus that the graph showing –5 is correct. Mr. Singh sketches both possibilities and puts a question mark beside the +5 version to indicate the class's hesitation.

Mr. Singh uses **inductive teaching** to offer another example: "Let's try one more. The football team loses 7 yards on a play. Make your sketch, then talk with your partner." He listens to the conversations in the room and asks a student to share his thinking. The student shows a graph displaying –7 and explains that he went that way (left or negative) because if you lose yards, you move away from the goal. "The goal must be moving forward (pointing right or positive) so this is moving backwards." Mr. Singh asks the class to signal thumbs up if they agree or thumbs down if they disagree. Although he's noticed some students changing their graphs, everyone signals thumbs up so Mr. Singh continues.

Inductive teaching utilizes several examples that require students to notice how a specific concept or concepts work.

EFFECT SIZE FOR PROVIDING FORMATIVE EVALUATION = 0.48

At this point, Mr. Singh tells the class the purpose of the lesson and reviews the success criteria. He clarifies the correct drawings for the two negative number situations as he explains how each of the four graphs from the opening activity shows a positive or negative number situation. Mr. Singh asks the students to talk in their small groups about the difference between the positive and negative number situations. He collects ideas from each small group and writes them on the board:

- Owing is the opposite of getting money.
- Moving forward is the opposite of moving backward.
- It's bad to owe money and good to get it.
- You'll lose if you move backward and win if you move forward.

Mr. Singh tells the students that one of the important ideas of negative numbers is that they are opposites of positive numbers. He introduces the vocabulary of *"the sign of the number is positive"* or *"the sign of the number is negative"* and helps the class make the connection to positive and negative as adjectives telling what kind of number. He knows the class has studied parts of speech in language arts and he is setting the stage for distinguishing between the signs of numbers and the operations addition and subtraction.

Instructional Approaches That Promote Conceptual Understanding

Mr. Singh pulls out two-color counters and distributes them to the class so each pair has a handful. Referring to the day's learning intention of representing integers on number lines and with two-color counters, he uses **direct/deliberate instruction** to teach students how to represent integers with two-color counters. Mr. Singh chose an inductive method for working on the number line because that representation is familiar to his students and they have had informal conversations about negative numbers on the number line. Two-color counters are an unfamiliar tool for integers, and a mini-lesson using deliberate instruction is an efficient way to introduce this new representation.

Knowing that deliberate instruction is not a synonym for lecture, Mr. Singh is careful in how he presents the material. The work with integers on number lines serves to create or activate students' prior knowledge of integers and whether situations are represented by positive or negative values. Mr. Singh introduces the new representation by telling the students that the convention is to use the color red to represent negative numbers: "Knowing this, you represent losing 7 yards using seven counters, for 7 yards, with the red side up because we're losing yardage." This careful language models the two elements of a signed number, quantity and sign. Students quickly select seven counters and place them red side up. Mr. Singh scans their work to confirm everyone is with him. He goes to the board and sketches beside the number line representing –7, telling the students that both representations show negative seven (Figure 3.8).

Teaching Takeaway

Teachers do not have to *start* each day or class period with the learning intentions and success criteria. They sometimes provide an engaging hook or introduction to the learning and then share the intentions and criteria for success later in the lesson.

> EFFECT SIZE FOR DIRECT/ DELIBERATE INSTRUCTION = 0.60

This is a **deliberate instruction** approach to teaching and learning mathematics.

TWO REPRESENTATIONS OF NEGATIVE SEVEN

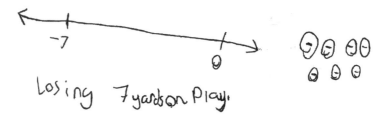

Figure 3.8

He guides the class through using the counters to create discrete representations for the other three situations the class has discussed. Mr. Singh circulates and provides students with feedback on their models. At the end of this practice session, he updates the sketches on the board. These will serve as worked examples for the independent practice to follow.

Mr. Singh shows a list on the screen of many different situations involving positive and negative numbers. Some continue the money and game themes already established, while others include temperature measured in Celsius. Mr. Singh instructs his students: "For each of these situations, create two models. One will be a number line and the other will use the two-color counters. Record both models in your math notebook." He circulates, questioning students about what in the situation tells them that the value is positive or negative and what tells them how far from zero the mark should be or how many counters should be used in the model. By asking these questions, he is laying the foundation for the idea of absolute value, separating distance or quantity from sign or direction.

As Mr. Singh observes his students, he checks off on his daily recording sheet that he has observed each student correctly representing integers using number lines and two-color counters. In this class, every student has been successful today, but two students were absent. The "A" penciled in beside their names is Mr. Singh's reminder to make time to address this content with these students when they return. Students who were not successful in the lesson today would have a notation of "–," a reminder for Mr. Singh to gather these students during intervention time for additional targeted practice.

As pairs successfully complete representing the situations on the screen, Mr. Singh gives each team a second assignment, this time on paper. He says, "This assignment asks you to move a step further in your thinking. Look at our fourth success criterion. This time you must compare the values to determine which one is greater or which one is less."

> EFFECT SIZE
> FOR DELIBERATE
> PRACTICE = **0.79**

> Represent each value using either a number line or two-color counters. Determine which value is greater. Explain how you know using your model.
>
> 1. The football team gained 4 yards on the first play. They lost 8 yards on the second play. Which play was best for the team?
>
> 2. The high temperature on January 3 was –5 degrees Celsius. The high temperature on January 10 was –8 degrees Celsius. Which day was warmer?

This time, students are asked to represent two situations using the method of their choice (number line or two-color counters) and determine which value is greater or which value is less. The students must explain their reasoning using their models.

Teaching for Clarity at the Close

To close the lesson, Mr. Singh asks students to share their thinking about the comparison problems. He confirms his observational data that students are able to correctly represent integers using one or both of the models he has provided. As he asks students to explain their comparisons, he highlights two important ideas that arise. First, the mathematics of comparison is not always framed as a "greater than or less than" question. In these problems, the questions are about the warmer day or the better play. Both of these represent the idea of finding the larger value of the two given. The class makes a list of many ways they might see the idea of comparison expressed in a variety of contexts.

Second, the class begins to notice patterns that are helpful in identifying the larger or smaller value. They realize first that they have always been comparing positive numbers so when both values are positive, nothing changes. Second, they realize that when they are comparing a positive and a negative value, the positive value is always greater. The challenge comes when they compare two negatives. At the end of class, students still have a difference of opinion when comparing −5 and −8. Some believe −5 degrees is the greater value because it's the warmer temperature (or, at least, less cold!), whereas others believe −8 is the greater value because 8 is greater than 5. Mr. Singh leaves the class with this difference of opinion and promises to continue the conversation tomorrow.

Mr. Singh is pleased with the progress his students have made. They have learned about the language and notation of representing positive and negative numbers in familiar contexts. He noticed that many students preferred to model integers with two-color counters, perhaps because this is a new tool for them and they like the hands-on engagement of working with the counters. He suspects this is part of the reason some students are still struggling with integer comparison when both values are negative. The consistency of "the larger value is further to the right on a traditional horizontal number line" is easier to see on a number line than when representing values with counters. This is one of the differences between these models and Mr. Singh will focus tomorrow's lesson on helping students make this connection. Figure 3.9 shows how Mr. Singh made his planning visible so that he could then provide an engaging and rigorous learning experience for his learners.

Mr. Singh's Teaching for Clarity PLANNING GUIDE

ESTABLISHING PURPOSE

1

What are the key content standards I will focus on in this lesson?

Content Standard (2016 Virginia SOLs):
  Virginia Standard of Learning 6.6
  The student will
  a. add, subtract, multiply, and divide integers;
  b. solve practical problems involving operations with integers; and
  c. simplify numerical expressions involving integers.

Mathematical Process Goal for Students:

- Mathematical representations

2

What are the learning intentions (the goal and *why* of learning, stated in student-friendly language) I will focus on in this lesson?

Content: I am learning to understand that real-world situations require positive and negative numbers.
Language: I am learning to use words (positive, negative, opposite, sign) and symbols (+, −) correctly when speaking and writing about positive and negative numbers.
Social: I am learning to work collaboratively with my partner to complete today's task.

3

When will I introduce and reinforce the learning intention(s) so that students understand it, see the relevance, connect it to previous learning, and can clearly communicate it themselves?

After the opening activity, students should think about opposites and see me record using appropriate language and notation before discussing the learning intention, so they have a model of what is expected in the learning intentions and success criteria.

SUCCESS CRITERIA

4   **What evidence shows that students have mastered the learning intention(s)? What criteria will I use?**

I can statements:

- I can correctly identify situations involving positive and/or negative numbers.
- I can represent the integers in a given problem on a number line.
- I can represent the values of a given situation using two-color counters.
- I can compare the values of positive and negative numbers.

5   **How will I check students' understanding (assess learning) during instruction and make accommodations?**

While my students collaborate on their models and sketches, they record the work in their own math notebook. My daily checklist will focus on correct use of the two representations so I know the students have mastered each model. I will circulate, questioning students about what in the situation tells them that the value is positive or negative and what tells them how far from zero the mark should be or how many counters should be used in the model. I want to lay the foundation for the idea of absolute value, separating distance or quantity from direction or sign.

The students will complete a second assignment introducing the idea of comparisons in the same contexts as they conclude the initial task.

INSTRUCTION

6   **What activities and tasks will move students forward in their learning?**

Using a familiar model (number lines), I will describe situations and challenge students to represent them on the number line. Some situations involve negative numbers.

After revealing the learning intention and success criteria, I will use deliberate instruction to show students how to model integers using counters as well.

Students work in pairs to model integer situations. As they gain confidence, I will introduce situations that ask questions about comparison (e.g., Which is larger/smaller?) with a particular focus on the number line model.

7   **What resources (materials and sentence frames) are needed?**

Number lines, two-color counters (or other discrete model), situations

8   **How will I organize and facilitate the learning? What questions will I ask? How will I initiate closure?**

Students will work with partners to model and discuss integers in a variety of familiar contexts, especially money, temperature, and sports.

Opening examples will get students thinking about opposites (I earned $5 versus I spent $5) and practice representing integers on the number line (a familiar context), and then reveal learning intentions and teach how to use discrete modeling tools (not as intuitive as number lines).

I will offer additional student practice with both models and then move to some comparison questions (e.g., Both teams lost yardage in the game. Who had the better/worse day?). If time permits, I will ask students to generalize about comparison rules.

online resources   This lesson plan is available for download at resources.corwin.com/vlmathematics-6-8.

Figure 3.9   Mr. Singh's Conceptual Understanding Lesson on Integers

Reflection

These three examples from Ms. Halstrom, Ms. Fernandez, and Mr. Singh exemplify teaching mathematics for conceptual understanding. As in the previous chapter, these three teachers selected a different approach or combination of approaches from the other two classrooms.

Using what you have read in this chapter, reflect on the following questions:

1. In your own words, describe what teaching for conceptual understanding looks like in your mathematics classroom.

2. How does the Teaching for Clarity Planning Guide support your intentionality in teaching for conceptual understanding?

3. Compare and contrast the approaches to teaching taken by the classroom teachers featured in this chapter.

4. Consider the following statement: *Conceptual understanding occurs as the surface, deep, and transfer phases of learning.* Do you agree or disagree with the statement? Why or why not? How is this statement reflected in this chapter?

5. How did the classroom teachers featured in this chapter adjust the difficulty and/or complexity of the mathematics tasks to meet the needs of all learners?

TEACHING FOR PROCEDURAL KNOWLEDGE AND FLUENCY 4

CHAPTER 4 SUCCESS CRITERIA:

(1) I can describe what teaching for procedural fluency in the mathematics classroom looks like.

(2) I can apply the Teaching for Clarity Planning Guide to teaching procedural skills.

(3) I can compare and contrast different approaches to teaching for procedural fluency with conceptual understanding and teaching for application.

(4) I can give examples of how to differentiate mathematics tasks designed for procedural knowledge.

Procedural fluency includes the ability to select, use, and transfer mathematics procedures in problem solving. Procedurally fluent learners know when one procedure is more appropriate than another one for a particular problem.

Teaching Takeaway

Procedural knowledge can be at the deep phase of learning. This occurs when learners make connections between specific procedures or skills in their mathematics learning.

EFFECT SIZE FOR PRIOR ABILITY = 0.94

In mathematics, you have to be able to solve problems. The successful teaching and learning of mathematics involves the execution of procedures that yield an expression, value, or set of values. Acquiring and consolidating procedural skills is a necessary aspect of mathematics if learners are to have the appropriate tools for taking on the next challenge in their learning progression. As we make our final visit to our three featured teachers, let's focus on the ways in which each teacher created learning experiences that allowed students to develop and practice the necessary procedural skills and progress toward **procedural fluency** with those skills. As you review these examples, we encourage you to take a look at the adjustments each teacher made to the learning experience so that students at the surface, deep, and transfer phases of learning could all engage in the mathematics task. And as before, you'll see how Ms. Halstrom, Ms. Fernandez, and Mr. Singh were able to differentiate the rigor of the mathematics tasks. Also, given the progression of middle school mathematics toward algebraic reasoning, the videos accessible through the QR codes accompanying this chapter are from an algebra classroom.

Ms. Halstrom and Circles and Cylinders

Ms. Halstrom's students are confident in their ability to find the circumference of a circle and they see the connection between this learning and their work on ratios and proportional relationships. This unit also expects students to find the area of circles and be able to explain the relationship between circumference and area. At the end of yesterday's lesson building fluency in finding the circumference of a circle, Ms. Halstrom used an exit ticket to assess how well her students remember and can use the formula for finding the area of parallelograms, an important aspect of today's lesson. All students could compute the area of a rectangular parallelogram; some struggled to compute the area of a parallelogram without right angles. Ms. Halstrom was pleased to see students using sketches of the parallelogram to reason about the answer. They remembered visually that they could slide a triangle from one side to the other and create a rectangle. The key idea is height and not side length, which allows the area of parallelograms to be calculated analogously to rectangles.

What Ms. Halstrom Wants Her Students to Learn

As with the previous lesson on circumference as a ratio, today's lesson will guide students through a structured exploration of the area of a circle. Ms. Halstrom will help students connect their thinking to the area of a parallelogram, which they already understand. Because students understand the concept of area in general, today's lesson focuses more on the particular procedures (namely, the area formula) used to calculate the area of a circle. Ms. Halstrom wants her students to understand where the formula comes from, and the standards expect this as well.

Because this lesson focuses on an informal derivation of the formula, mathematical practices are front and center in this lesson. Ms. Halstrom emphasizes the third Standard for Mathematical Practice (construct viable arguments and critique the reasoning of others) when she expects her students to clearly explain their reasoning and understand (and critique) the reasoning of their classmates.

Ms. Halstrom knows this will be a challenging lesson and that she will need to work to keep productive struggle from tipping into unproductive struggle and frustration. She is working with the following standards:

MATHEMATICS CONTENT AND PRACTICE STANDARDS

7.G.B

Solve real-life and mathematical problems involving angle measure, area, surface area, and volume.

7.G.B.4

Know the formulas for the area and circumference of a circle and use them to solve problems; give an informal derivation of the relationship between the circumference and area of a circle.

7.EE.A.1

Apply properties of operations as strategies to add, subtract, factor, and expand linear expressions with rational coefficients.

(Continued)

> (Continued)
>
> **Ms. Halstrom is helping her learners develop the following Standard for Mathematical Practice:**
>
> • Construct viable arguments and critique the reasoning of others.

EFFECT SIZE
FOR PROVIDING
FORMATIVE
EVALUATION = 0.48

Focusing this lesson on constructing arguments means Ms. Halstrom will devote her attention to eliciting and using evidence of student thinking. This is how she will know the argument students are constructing and how well they understand the relationship between the area and circumference of a circle. In more advanced geometry classes, students might construct proofs as evidence of understanding. In this seventh grade class, verbal reasoning is highlighted as students explain their thinking clearly and make their case for the relationship under investigation.

Learning Intentions and Success Criteria

Video 10
Differentiating Instruction to Support Surface, Deep, and Transfer Learning

https://resources.corwin.com/vlmathematics-6-8

Ms. Halstrom designed this procedural lesson with a focus on both developing an understanding of why and how the procedure works, as well as providing students opportunities to practice carrying out the procedure. In addition to the procedure about finding the area of a circle, the lesson also provides an opportunity for students to practice the procedures of a second content standard: Applying properties of operations as strategies to add, subtract, factor, and expand linear expressions with rational coefficients. While the final expression will not be linear, Ms. Halstrom values the practice opportunity this task provides.

EFFECT SIZE
FOR TEACHER
CLARITY = 0.75

> *Content Learning Intention:* I am learning to develop an understanding of the area formula for circles.
>
> *Language Learning Intention:* I am learning to use appropriate vocabulary and notation when communicating our thinking about circles.
>
> *Social Learning Intention:* I am learning to support the explanation of the relationship between circumference and area in a circle using dialogue and thoughtful questioning.

Ms. Halstrom has focused her success criteria for this lesson in three areas. First, students must decompose a circle into smaller parts that can be organized into a parallelogram. They use this figure to explain the relationship between the circumference and area of the circle. Students will explain their arguments more clearly if they use correct vocabulary so this is specifically called out in the language learning intention, which also references notation for written work. Finally, Ms. Halstrom has made explicit the expectation that students will create convincing arguments for the relationship between area and circumference as a social learning intention. The success criteria for today's lesson are as follows:

> EFFECT SIZE FOR COGNITIVE TASK ANALYSIS = 1.29

- ☐ I can rearrange parts of a circle to form a shape whose area I know.
- ☐ I can identify the radius and circumference of the original circle in the new figure.
- ☐ I can tell how to find the area of the new shape using the dimensions of the circle.
- ☐ I can explain the relationship between the circumference and area of the circle.
- ☐ I can calculate the area of a circle when I know the radius or diameter.

Ms. Halstrom has been working with her students on constructing arguments using the strategy "convince yourself, convince a friend, convince a skeptic" (Boaler & Humpreys, 2005). The students are good at convincing themselves they are correct and are now working to convince their peers. Peers are encouraged to ask questions of each other to clarify points of an argument and make the language more precise. An important part of today's lesson is giving students the opportunity to practice making an effective argument and to practice asking good questions while listening to a peer's argument.

> EFFECT SIZE FOR ASSESSMENT-CAPABLE VISIBLE LEARNERS = 1.33

> EFFECT SIZE FOR HELP SEEKING = 0.72

Guiding and Scaffolding Student Thinking

As class begins, Ms. Halstrom shows the class a circle on the screen and asks how they might find the area. Students are encouraged to brainstorm with shoulder partners and select their best strategy. Ms. Halstrom uses this particular approach at this specific time because her learners

Video 11
Supporting Surface
Learning Needs With a
Peer Tutor

*https://resources.corwin.com/
vlmathematics-6-8*

EFFECT SIZE
FOR STRATEGY
MONITORING
= 0.58

have demonstrated their fluency with the technical language needed to engage in this brainstorm. As Ms. Halstrom circulates throughout the room, she finds that some students are aware of a formula and she encourages them to reason about the problem for now. She selects three groups to share their strategies and invites them to present in a deliberate sequence. She believes that sequencing student sharing is important; she doesn't want the "perfect answer" to come first so students can hear the good elements of work from a number of students. This approach is not about highlighting those that know. Ms. Halstrom wants to highlight the good thinking of those who are working well but haven't gotten to the solution yet. This gives learners room to share their thinking and see it extended by their peers.

The first group to share has the idea of placing a grid over the circle and trying to count squares. This works for a part of the circle but becomes messy near the edges. The second group wonders about placing a circle in a square and figuring out what fraction of the area of the square (easy to calculate) the area of the circle represents. They too are bogged down in the details. The third group came to Ms. Halstrom's attention when they asked for a pair of scissors. As she declined the request, Ms. Halstrom asked what they were thinking about. When she heard their idea, she asked them to share their thinking without testing their conjecture. This third group wanted to trim the circle into rectangles and rearrange the pieces to make it into a figure whose area they did know.

As she anticipated student responses during planning, Ms. Halstrom thought about what strategies she had seen students use in previous years as well as interesting responses to this task she had heard from colleagues. She was confident she would have some students use the idea of counting a grid. She also suspected some would try partitioning the square into pieces whose area they knew; the idea of placing the circle in a square was a variation of this thinking. Ms. Halstrom hoped at least one group would take this idea further and want to rearrange the pieces of the circle, the very activity she had planned for class today. As part of her planning, Ms. Halstrom had decided to sequence sharing in this way, allowing the most basic strategy of counting squares to come first and ending with the strategy that feeds her lesson best. Alongside purposeful planning of questions, Ms. Halstrom finds this exercise of anticipating student responses and sequencing how they might be shared (Smith & Stein, 2011) one of the most productive parts of her planning.

The class is comfortable with the way Ms. Halstrom asks them to share and they have learned to build on each other's thinking as they share. The second group to share recognized that their problem was essentially the same as that of the first group. The third group commented, "We plan to cut out the rectangles and then think these pieces (motioning to the curved areas at the outer edge of the circle) might go together to make more rectangles." Ms. Halstrom also coaches her students to ask questions when they do not see connections between their own thinking and the thinking of others. She keeps sentence frames on a board in the room to help with these discussions. Students can use structures such as "I understand _____ but do not understand how you connected _____ to _____." Those questions can help us identify gaps in reasoning or understanding, she says, and that makes our arguments better.

EFFECT SIZE FOR STUDENT SELF-VERBALIZATION AND SELF-QUESTIONING = 0.55

Instructional Approaches That Promote Procedural Fluency

Ms. Halstrom reviews the learning intentions and success criteria with the class. She emphasizes that they must know both the formula and where it comes from. Today's lesson will start with figuring out where the formula comes from. Ms. Halstrom asks the class to distribute the fraction circle sets at their tables. They will be working with shoulder partners today, so there are two circle sets per table of four. Each group will need the whole along with the eighths, tenths, and twelfths. She draws their attention to the whole first, telling the class that the challenge today is to find the area of this circle: "We are going to use a strategy like the one just shared to find the area of this circle. These pieces are already cut into wedge shapes. Your challenge is to use these wedges to build a shape whose area you know how to find. I suggest you start with the fourths. Remember to use all four and not to use pieces from a second circle." Giving students time to work, she moves about the room listening to the discussion and watching students work. Many students make one of the shapes as seen here and begin to discuss what to call it.

EFFECT SIZE FOR
QUESTIONING
= 0.48

Teaching Takeaway

We must map out and plan the questions we plan to ask students during the lesson. The focus of those questions should be to move student thinking forward in mathematics.

Some students want to consider it a rectangle but there's a problem with the curved sides. Others struggle because they cannot find the right angles a rectangle requires. As she circulates throughout the room, Ms. Halstrom asks groups to show her where the radius and circumference of the original circle appear in the figures they are creating, knowing this will be essential as they move forward. For students who struggle, she asks them a question: "If you put the circle back together, can you find the radius and circumference? What strategy could you use to keep track of these parts as you rearrange your circle?" This helps students learn to find these components even when the circle does not look like a circle.

As pairs show comfort with the components of the figure, Ms. Halstrom encourages them to build similar figures using the other sets of pieces. As students create each variation, she challenges them to locate the radius and circumference, reminding them that the radius does not have to be along the edge of a piece. These are the prompts and scaffolded comments that she planned purposefully as she designed the lesson. She knew students would be most confident tracking the radius as one of the straight edges of the fraction circle piece. Yet knowing that does not confirm that students understand the radius is *any* segment from the center of the circle to the edge. The point of the wedge is the center of the circle (hence her decision to use commercial or die-cut fraction circles rather than having students cut them), and the radius is any segment from the center to the edge. The questions did not require planning because they were difficult to think of. Rather, they required planning so Ms. Halstrom would ask them at the right time for maximum impact on student thinking.

As the class works through building the figures, Ms. Halstrom asks them to start describing their shape to their partner using this sentence frame: "This figure looks like a _____ to me because I see _____, _____, and _____." She reminds the students that exactly three elements are not required and then returns them to their partners to describe their figures. This is the first step of the argument.

As Ms. Halstrom hears some of the discussion settle on non-rectangular parallelograms as the name of the figure, she asks each group of students to think about how they could find the area of the shape. Based on the circle, can they figure out the length of the base and the height? Where teams cannot resolve the name of the figure, she asks students if they think the left and right sides would ever be perfectly vertical and perpendicular to the base. While some students can see that with skinny enough wedges it would get close, this helps them recognize that they cannot get there with the pieces they have. Again, planning questions and prompts serve Ms. Halstrom and her students well.

Earlier in the process, most students realized that the curved edges forming the top and bottom of the parallelogram were the circumference of the circle. The curves made this easy to track. Some students also noticed that the top and bottom of the figure became straighter as the wedges were smaller. A few groups stacked one figure on top of another to realize that they were still generally the same size—the area of the circle was still there.

Ms. Halstrom challenges each pair to tell how they would calculate the area of the parallelogram in terms of the radius and circumference of the circle. This is the second step of their informal argument about the formula for area of a circle. As Ms. Halstrom circulates throughout the room, she keeps asking students what they need to know (the length of the base and the height of the figure) and how the circle can help them find these things. The length of the base is half the circumference (half the wedges are pointed up and half pointed down in each figure) and the height is the radius, dropping from the point of the wedge (the center of the circle)

EFFECT SIZE FOR
CONCEPTUAL
CHANGE
PROGRAMS = 0.99

EFFECT SIZE FOR
SCAFFOLDING
= 0.82

EFFECT SIZE FOR
PLANNING AND
PREDICTION = 0.76

Teaching Takeaway

Deliberate instruction through a mini-lesson can take place at any point during the instructional block. Again, it's really about the right approach at the right time for student learning.

roughly perpendicular to the (pretend it's perfectly straight) base. She encourages partners to explain the connections they see to each other using a common structure:

> I rearranged the pieces of the circle into a _____. I know it's a _____ because _____. I can find the area of _____ by doing this (applying the known formula) and naming the dimensions based on their role in the circle (radius or circumference).

As Ms. Halstrom watches her class, she knows some students are reaching the edge of productive struggle. These are the students for whom algebraic procedures and language are still difficult, and this challenge pushes their thinking. With the most difficult algebra still to come, it is time to pull a small group together for some teacher-led instruction. Leaving most of the class to continue practicing their arguments on their own, Ms. Halstrom meets with three pairs of students as a group. She begins by drawing a non-rectangular parallelogram on a small dry-erase board and asking a student how to find the area of the figure. Laying the board down, she has a student place the "parallelogram from a circle" beside it and Ms. Halstrom briefly thinks aloud using the sentence frames she provided earlier:

> I rearranged the pieces of the circle into a parallelogram. I know it's a parallelogram because I see two pairs of parallel sides (motioning to the figure). There are no right angles so this is not a rectangle. I can find the area of the parallelogram by multiplying the base by the height (again motioning to the figure). The height of the parallelogram is the radius of the circle and the base is half of the circumference of the circle.

These students need the additional support of this teacher-led example. Having shared her thinking, Ms. Halstrom has the students turn to each other to practice the argument before dismissing her small group.

Because the activity is taking longer than expected, Ms. Halstrom decides to lead the class through the algebraic part of the argument together. She gives the students time to finish their current thought and pulls the class together. She asks a student to state the argument so far, and the student makes her thinking visible with this explanation:

> I rearranged the 12 pieces of the circle into a shape like a parallelogram. If I pretend the top and bottom are straight, they would be parallel to each other. The angled sides are parallel to each other. There aren't any right angles, so this is a parallelogram that isn't a rectangle. The area of a parallelogram is base times height. You have to remember that base isn't this (pointing to the angled side) but this (motioning a segment perpendicular to the base). These two sides (top and bottom) are the circumference of the circle with the curves, so the base is half of the circumference. This height is still the radius of the circle because it goes from the point (the center) to the curved edge. So the area is one-half times the circumference times the radius.

Ms. Halstrom reminds students that explaining the relationship between circumference and area was one of their success criteria. She writes the equation just named on the board and then asks them to turn to their partners and restate the claim in their own words. She uses this opportunity to scan the room and listen to peer conversations (*Are they minding the language learning intention, the social learning intention, and understanding the content?*).

Ms. Halstrom writes the following equation on the board: $A = \left(\frac{1}{2}\right)C \times r$. She asks, "Do we know another expression equivalent to C (circumference)?" The students recognize this as a chance to use what they had practiced the day before: C is equal to π times the diameter. The teacher asks, "Is there another way to say this, maybe using the radius? Remember you had some problems like this." That is the nudge the class needs to see that C is also equal to π times twice the radius. Ms. Halstrom writes $C = 2\pi r$ on the board under the first equation.

"How can we use these together? Talk to your partner."

The class connects the two by substitution: $A = \left(\frac{1}{2}\right)(2\pi r)(r)$. Ms. Halstrom leads them through simplifying the expression ($A = \pi r^2$) and connects this example with a variable to the work they did with exponents in Grade 6.

Teaching Takeaway

An exit ticket provides a formative evaluation of student learning.

Teaching for Clarity at the Close

Ms. Halstrom reminds the class of the success criteria for the day. Students are confident of the reasoning part of the lesson and now it is time for practice. Ms. Halstrom distributes a short practice page with six problems asking students to calculate the area of a circle. For four problems, students are given the radius of a circle and asked to use the formula. For the final two problems, the diameter is given. The students pull out their calculators and start to work. Ms. Halstrom will use this information to determine how much additional practice her students need in applying the formula.

At the end of the day, Ms. Halstrom stopped to think about how the lesson had gone across all her classes. The algebra had pushed her students. She knew that it would and she had prepared for that in planning her questions and being ready to pull the class together at the end. She was pleased that her students could use the structure she provided for the argument and that they were asking good clarifying questions of each other. She could hear her own voice in some of the questions: "Can you say that again using our math vocabulary?" or "I don't follow how you got from here to here. Can you tell me again with more details?" This meant her work asking questions in consistent ways was paying off as students internalized these ways of thinking and questioning.

Ms. Halstrom also reviewed her students' practice work applying the formula for area of a circle. Most of the students were successful and were ready for this skill to slip into the ongoing spaced practice she used for homework. There are a few students she will need to pull aside during Friday's extra help period, so she made a note to put that on the schedule. She will create a worked example for these students during this time. Figure 4.1 shows how Ms. Halstrom made her planning visible so that she could then provide an engaging and rigorous learning experience for her learners.

Ms. Halstrom's Teaching for Clarity PLANNING GUIDE

ESTABLISHING PURPOSE

1

What are the key content standards I will focus on in this lesson?

Content Standards:

7.G.B

Solve real-life and mathematical problems involving angle measure, area, surface area, and volume.

7.G.B.4

Know the formulas for the area and circumference of a circle and use them to solve problems; give an informal derivation of the relationship between the circumference and area of a circle.

7.EE.A.1

Apply properties of operations as strategies to add, subtract, factor, and expand linear expressions with rational coefficients.

Standard for Mathematical Practice:

• Construct viable arguments and critique the reasoning of others.

2

What are the learning intentions (the goal and *why* of learning stated in student-friendly language) I will focus on in this lesson?

Content: I am learning to develop an understanding of the area formula for circles.

Language: I am learning to use appropriate vocabulary and notation when communicating our thinking about circles.

Social: I am learning to support the explanation of the relationship between circumference and area in a circle using dialogue and thoughtful questioning.

3 When will I introduce and reinforce the learning intention(s) so that students understand it, see the relevance, connect it to previous learning, and can clearly communicate it themselves?

I will introduce the learning intentions in the middle of the lesson, after students have constructed their parallelograms (and see the relationship generally) and before beginning work on the formula. This allows them to discover the big idea of the lesson and gives purpose for moving to the more procedural element, finding the formula.

SUCCESS CRITERIA

4 What evidence shows that students have mastered the learning intention(s)? What criteria will I use?

I can statements:

- I can rearrange parts of a circle to form a shape whose area I know.

- I can identify the radius and circumference of the original circle in the new figure.

- I can tell how to find the area of the new shape using the dimensions of the circle.

- I can explain the relationship between the circumference and area of the circle.

- I can calculate the area of a circle when I know the radius or diameter.

5 How will I check students' understanding (assess learning) during instruction and make accommodations?

I will observe the following:

- Students creating "parallelograms" appropriately and finding the radius and circumference of the starting circle on their figure.
- Students using the formula for area of a parallelogram correctly.
- Students explaining their steps in deriving the formula for the area of a circle.

I will provide peer support if needed. This part is also less important as long as students can apply the formula and describe where it comes from.

I will see that students recognize closer approximations of a parallelogram with smaller wedges of the circle.

INSTRUCTION

6 What activities and tasks will move students forward in their learning?

I will discuss area of a circle and how counting squares isn't an easy strategy here. I will provide fraction circle pieces and have students explore constructing "parallelograms" with the pieces. I will move toward seeing that the height of the figure is the radius and the length of the base is half the circumference.

I will share the learning intention at this point and move toward deriving the formula. Depending on time and class energy, this part may be more deliberate instruction. I will allow practice at the end using the formula to find the area of several circles.

7

What resources (materials and sentence frames) are needed?

1. Fraction circles (at least wholes, fourths, and eighths; tenths or twelfths are helpful as well)

2. Calculators

8

How will I organize and facilitate the learning? What questions will I ask? How will I initiate closure?

1. Students will work in pairs to create their figures and share understanding through groups of four. I will ask the following questions:

   - Where do you see the circumference and radius of the circle in your figure?

   - How does your figure change when you have more wedges?

   - How can we use what you've done to find a formula for the area of a circle?

2. Closure brings the focus back to using the formula correctly with a brief practice session, extending into homework if necessary.

 This lesson plan is available for download at resources.corwin.com/vlmathematics-6-8.

Figure 4.1   Ms. Halstrom's Procedural Lesson on Circles and Cylinders

Ms. Fernandez and Systems of Linear Equations

The students in Ms. Fernandez's class were largely successful in developing a conceptual understanding of solutions to systems of equations in their previous lessons. She feels confident that her students have the foundation required for today's lesson, which is focused on building procedural knowledge, to take root and have meaning. Today, students will be graphing systems of linear equations as a means of approximating their solutions. Most of her students demonstrated some level of mastery of graphing linear equations by the end of their last unit. Graphing did prove more challenging for some students, however. Ms. Fernandez designed this lesson with all students in mind and decided to revisit these skills explicitly. She is comfortable with this decision because she knows that **spaced practice** has a relatively high effect size, and that is exactly what this revisiting will be for many of her students. Additionally, this will give her the space that she needs to provide some explicit reteaching for students who struggled more severely with graphing during the last unit.

What Ms. Fernandez Wants Her Students to Learn

Ms. Fernandez's lesson today will focus on students using their ability to explain that intersections of functions signify their solutions—a

> EFFECT SIZE FOR USE OF CALCULATORS = 0.27

Teaching Takeaway

Although the effect size for the use of calculators is < 0.40, when integral to the learning the effect size increases.

> EFFECT SIZE FOR SPACED VS. MASS PRACTICE = 0.60

Spaced practice is practice that occurs over time rather than in a single setting or practice session.

MATHEMATICS CONTENT AND PRACTICE STANDARDS

8.EE.C.8

Analyze and solve pairs of simultaneous linear equations.

b. . . . Estimate solutions [of a system] by graphing the equations.

Ms. Fernandez is helping her learners develop the following Standards for Mathematical Practice:

- Make sense of problems and persevere in solving them.
- Use appropriate tools strategically.
- Reason abstractly and quantitatively.

concept developed in previous lessons—in order to know *which* values to estimate.

Learning Intentions and Success Criteria

As usual, Ms. Fernandez begins her lesson by sharing the learning intentions with her students:

Content Learning Intention: I am learning to use our understanding of graphing linear functions as a means of solving systems of equations.

Language Learning Intention: I am learning to communicate the solutions to systems of equations verbally and in writing.

Social Learning Intention: I am learning to transition smoothly between roles during conversation roundtable.

Ms. Fernandez elaborates on the language and social learning intentions to explain the flow of the day to her students. She informs them that they will start by taking some notes on the new content: then they will practice the new skills, and finally they will engage in a collaborative task where they can practice in teams. On days like today when new procedural skills are being taught, Ms. Fernandez likes to remind her students, "Today is about learning new skills. We are going to get things wrong—we *should* get things wrong! It is okay because today we are practicing. You're supposed to make mistakes when you're practicing." She hopes that her traditional design to today's lesson will help facilitate those mistakes in a positive way that keeps learning moving forward. After all, direct instruction of this type has a relatively large effect size due to its deliberate design.

> EFFECT SIZE
> FOR NOTE TAKING
> = 0.50

> EFFECT SIZE
> FOR DIRECT/
> DELIBERATE
> INSTRUCTION
> = 0.60

Ms. Fernandez introduces the success criteria she wrote for today's lesson immediately after introducing the learning intentions. She writes the success criteria under the lesson heading in her "master notebook," which she has projected under a document camera. As she talks through them, students copy them down in their own notebooks. They recognize this protocol from their direct/deliberate instruction days and understand they will be redirected to these *I can* statements as part of a daily wrap-up. She includes some success criteria with the word *still* to remind them that they are using previously mastered learning.

> ☐ I can (still) graph linear equations.
> ☐ I can approximate solutions to systems of equations by creating graphs.
> ☐ I can explain solutions to systems of equations in writing.

Ms. Fernandez makes a point of emphasizing the word *still* in the first success criterion to signify to students that they are revisiting skills that they have previously developed. She writes *I can still* statements like these whenever she is calling on heavy doses of prior knowledge in order to propel a new lesson. She recognizes this type of learning as near transfer within mathematics, whereby students utilize preexisting mathematical structures in their mind's eye to access new, now-within-reach, mathematical constructs. Essentially, students will be using the math they own—which is graphing linear equations in this case—to make sense of the math they don't yet own—which in this case is solving systems of linear equations by graphing. If mathematical prerequisites exist for new learning to occur, then near transfer within mathematics is on the horizon.

Another reason that Ms. Fernandez chooses to address prior knowledge in specific lessons, and chooses to do so through the use of *I can still* statements, is to continually imprint another one of her mantras—namely, "Mastery requires maintenance." She communicates to her students that learning math is like riding a bike. The basic competency can never be taken away.

> Once you can ride a bike, you can always ride a bike. However, what happens if you don't ride your bike for a long time? What does it feel like when you hop back on? Are you as good as you used to be? Math is the same. If you want to get good, it requires practice and use. If you want to stay good, it requires practice and use. This, students, is because mastery requires maintenance.

She likes to share examples of this from her own learning experiences.

> One of the hardest classes I ever took in college was a physics class. After the first assessment, the professor handed our papers back with a number at the top next to our name—that number

**Teaching
Takeaway**

Teacher credibility
involves three
constructs:
competence,
trustworthiness,
and caring.

**Teaching
Takeaway**

Activating prior
knowledge is
important in
acquiring and
consolidating new
learning.

represented our score on the assessment. The number on my paper was a 42. Thinking that the number represented the points I had earned out of a total of 50, I was quite pleased with my performance. Unfortunately, the 42 was out of a possible 100 points. I had to work very hard to fill in the gaps in my learning and earned a B by the end of the semester. I had to do a lot of practice or maintenance to get to mastery in that class. If I took that very same final exam today, I would probably not do so well. I wouldn't get that same B. You know why?

Her students respond, "Because mastery requires maintenance."

Sharing real stories from her own life doesn't just build positive relationships with her students; it builds credibility. Ms. Fernandez is respected by her students and they regard her as a credible academic.

Modeling Strategies and Skills

Now that the purpose of the day is clear to her students and they know that they are required to bring prior knowledge to this new learning, Ms. Fernandez begins activating that knowledge. She says, "Students, last lesson we talked about the concept of a solution to a system of equations. Remind me, what is a solution to a system?" Ms. Fernandez takes a number of responses—even after hearing what she was looking for—to engage as many students as possible in this collective think-aloud. She reiterates a few responses that touched on the concept as being "the place on the graph where both equations have the same values."

"Okay," she continues, "so how were we able to know when two equations had the same value? How could we tell?"

One student raises her hand and responds with "Well, we could see it on the graph."

"Can you tell me more about that?" Ms. Fernandez uses an open-ended question to elicit further elaboration from her student.

"Well, if the lines touch, then they are the same point."

"What values would be the same?" Ms. Fernandez asks for clarification. This causes the student to pause briefly as other hands start to shoot up around her. "Hold on," Ms. Fernandez requests of her other eager students. "She'll ask for help if she needs it."

Ms. Fernandez knows this thoughtful advocacy will go a long way in developing both this student's agency and the culture of the classroom—thinking is not a race.

The student suddenly perks up and claims, "Both of them! They have to have the same *x* and *y*."

"Do we agree?" Ms. Fernandez looks around as the students display general concurrence.

Ms. Fernandez says, "You're absolutely right. What do we call it when graphs touch in math? What's the math language we have for this?" To link today's learning with prior learning, she projects the system of equations from a previous lesson (Figure 4.2).

Ms. Fernandez finds this to be an appropriate space to build her students' attention to precision with mathematical vocabulary, using a

EFFECT SIZE FOR
VOCABULARY
INSTRUCTION
= 0.62

SYSTEM OF LINEAR EQUATIONS: MOVIE PRICES

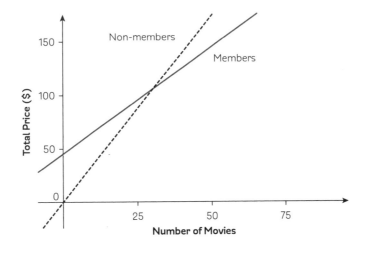

Figure 4.2

familiar context to do it. She hears a lot of *intersect* and *intersection* being called out, so she comfortably moves on. "Okay, so we know how to find a solution based on the graph of the two equations. Let's see if this can help with our first example."

With that, Ms. Fernandez writes down the equations associated with the graph from the previous lesson and the instructions for Example 1 in her projected notebook: *Approximate the solution to the following system of equations.*

$$C = 0.01m \qquad C = 40 + 0.02m$$

She first explains the context of these two equations: "You are comparing two different mobile phone plans. The first plan charges 10 cents per minute. The second plan charges a base fee of $40.00 plus 2 cents per minute." She then asks, "So how could we use what we know to help us with this new kind of problem? Were we given a table of data or a graph?" She pauses for effect. "No, hmm . . . So what can we do? Do either of these look familiar to us?" Students point out to her that the first one "looks like $y = mx$, [but] there is no intercept" and the second looks like "the normal $y = mx + b$." Recognizing this as her cue to begin teacher-modeling so that she can again help students attend to precision with their mathematical language, Ms. Fernandez jumps into action.

"I love how you are all looking for familiar structures in these equations—and you're right. This top equation is in slope-intercept form with an intercept of 0." Ms. Fernandez explicitly points at the coefficient 0.10 as she says *slope* and the empty space next to it as she says *with an intercept of 0.* "And this bottom one with a smaller slope is also in slope-intercept form and has a y-intercept of 40," she says as she uses two fingers to point at the y-intercept embedded in the second equation and gesture at the slope. Her goal in combining gestures with verbal descriptions is to connect the description of each equation with its meaning. She wants to imprint on her students that precise mathematical language is actually a tool that alludes to the meaning of mathematical structures and is not just confusing new jargon.

> We have used both of those to graph lines in the past. I am also recognizing that since I know how to graph these equations, I can use their graphs to find their intersection and approximate it to give me the solution. So let's graph! With the first one, what's my slope and how do you know?

Video 12
Checking for Understanding as Procedural Knowledge Deepens

https://resources.corwin.com/ vlmathematics-6-8

Ms. Fernandez jumps back into questioning as the driver of today's learning, since she is now addressing skills that students have previously built. She continues in this way to introduce the rest of the day's content, including graphing lines in other forms, approximating solutions to systems by examining their graphs, and explaining those solutions in writing.

Teaching in this style requires more than just a lesson plan; it also requires a sense of direction. This is where teacher clarity comes in. Ms. Fernandez knows where her students are, she knows which prior knowledge she wishes to access, and she knows where she wants her students to go. This provides her the freedom to open her classroom up—even during focused instruction as described above—and allow her students to openly explore their thinking when developing procedural skills. Through this, they discover the need for and the utility of procedural skills—not just their mere existence. It is plain to see, then, that clarity is a foundation and prerequisite to many other influences on learning.

> EFFECT SIZE FOR
> TEACHER CLARITY
> = 0.75

Guiding and Scaffolding Student Thinking

Ms. Fernandez provides a few examples similar to the one she modeled for students to engage in semi-independently. She also brings up a second example from a previous lesson: the nickels and dimes example. In this situation, the equations are in standard form and require additional work to graph. This means that students try to do what they can but are welcome and encouraged to refer to their notes and talk to partners to get needed boosts. Ms. Fernandez uses this time to sit with students she notices having difficulties graphing (some of whom she anticipated from their struggles during the last unit). During this guided practice phase, Ms. Fernandez uses questioning strategies much like those she uses during the whole-class discussions. The key difference, however, is that these questions are individualized for the student in front of her as she works diligently to understand how the student is accessing the content.

> EFFECT SIZE FOR
> REHEARSAL AND
> MEMORIZATION
> = 0.73

Ms. Fernandez comfortably diverts from the assigned problem once she is able to formatively assess which key concepts are causing students to struggle. For instance, as she notices one student graphing y-intercepts as x-intercepts instead, she discusses the concept with the student and generates additional mini-examples to build fluency. "Think about this equation: $y = x + 1$. What's the value of y when x is zero? What are the coordinates of that point?" she asks.

The student responds with, "y is 1, so the point is (0, 1)."

"Right. What about the equation $y = 2x + 3$? What is the value of y when x is zero?"

The student responds with, "y is 3, so the point is (0, 3)." They repeat this conversation for several more examples.

The teacher continues, "What pattern do you notice about the coordinates of the point and the constant in the equation?"

"If x is zero, the y coordinate is always the constant."

"Now let's think about graphing these equations. Where would these points [gesturing to the list of (0, b) coordinates the student has made] appear on a graph?"

"They all have zeros, so on an axis."

"Great. Which axis?" Ms. Fernandez asks. The student seems unsure of the question's wording as he looks at her with a "right-in-front-of-you-on-the-paper" sort of look. Ms. Fernandez recognizes this expression and rephrases her question in the moment. "Where are the zeros? Are they always x-values, always y-values, or both in these examples?"

"Oh! The x is always zero, so I don't move side to side. They're all on the y-axis."

"There we go. So what do we call this point (gesturing to the b value in one of the equations)?"

"The y-intercept on the vertical axis," the student says as he points to the vertical axis to emphasize his understanding, "and x is always zero."

"Wonderful! Now let's try your graphs again with that perspective." Ms. Fernandez stays with the student and works through graphing the second example (Figure 4.3).

Guided practice is key for students as they reach for the limits of their "zones of proximal development," as Vygotsky would put it. The zone

SYSTEM OF LINEAR EQUATIONS: NICKELS AND DIMES

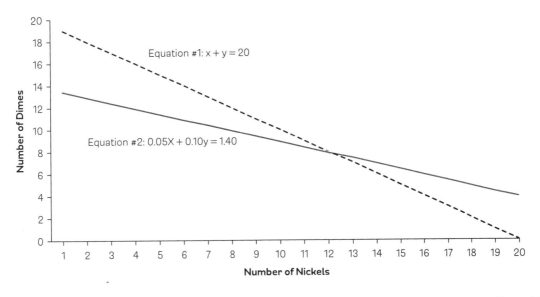

Figure 4.3

of proximal development is the current upper bound of new learning that students can reach with the right help. Vygotsky defines the zone of proximal development as "the distance between the actual development level as determined by independent problem solving and the level of potential development as determined through problem solving under adult guidance or in collaboration with more capable peers" (Cole, John-Steiner, Scribner, & Souberman, 1978, p. 86). Essentially, the zone of proximal development is what an individual is ready to learn. It is measured as the difference between what an individual can do alone and what he or she can do with support. During guided practice, the teacher is that support.

Instructional Approaches That Promote Procedural Fluency

Ms. Fernandez continues the lesson by encouraging students to share their work under the document camera and verbally annotate their

EFFECT SIZE FOR TEACHING STRATEGIES = 0.57

EFFECT SIZE FOR RECIPROCAL TEACHING = 0.74

thinking as they proceed through each step. Students identify and justify each decision they made along the solution path—much like a think-aloud. What Ms. Fernandez finds wonderful about this process is that while she catches students emulating some of her strategies and explanations (which warms her heart), she also hears them explain their thinking: "The way *I* see it . . ." or "*I* think about it kind of like . . ." This ownership of the material from peers can help connect students to the content on a different level. Sometimes, Ms. Fernandez recognizes, they can't necessarily see themselves in the head of the teacher as they can see themselves in the head of their peers, further echoing the need for *collaboration with more capable peers* as previously identified by Vygotsky (Cole et al., 1978).

Now that students have had opportunities to see how their teacher approaches these procedural skills, they have heard how their peers think through problems of this type, and they have had time to practice building their own skillsets, Ms. Fernandez has planned for them to engage in a collaborative task. She places students into groups of four and provides each student a sheet of graph paper. She prompts them to fold the paper into a conversation roundtable foldable (Figures 4.4 through 4.6).

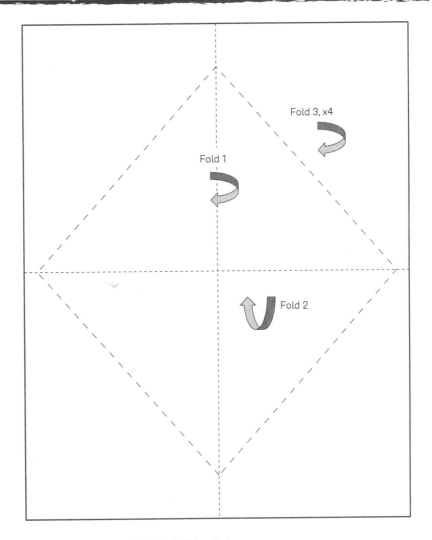

1. Fold in half lengthwise.
2. Fold in half widthwise.
3. Fold each corner toward center.

Source: Adapted from Fisher, 2017.

Figure 4.4

 A template for a conversation roundtable foldable is available for download at resources.corwin.com/vlmathematics-6-8.

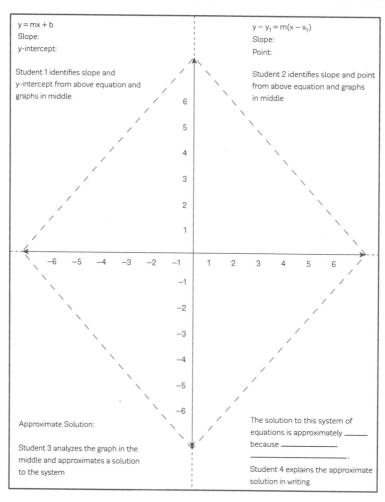

$y = mx + b$
Slope:
y-intercept:

Student 1 identifies slope and y-intercept from above equation and graphs in middle

$y - y_1 = m(x - x_1)$
Slope:
Point:

Student 2 identifies slope and point from above equation and graphs in middle

Approximate Solution:

Student 3 analyzes the graph in the middle and approximates a solution to the system

The solution to this system of equations is approximately _____ because _____ _____.

Student 4 explains the approximate solution in writing.

Source: Adapted from Fisher, 2017.

Figure 4.5

She then asks students to label each quadrant with the following words, starting on the upper quadrant.

Quadrant 1: Equation: Slope: y-intercept:

Quadrant 2: Equation: Slope: point:

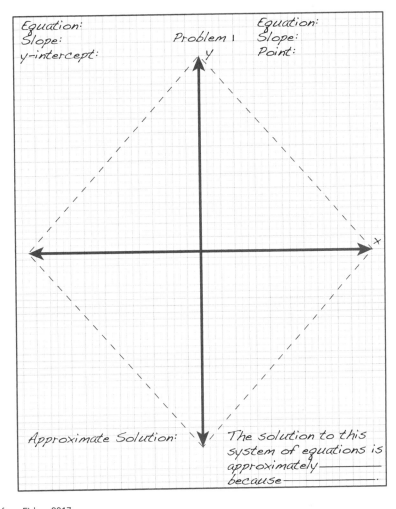

Source: Adapted from Fisher, 2017.

Figure 4.6

Quadrant 3: Approximate Solution:

Quadrant 4: Explanation: The solution to this system of equations is approximately _____ because _____.

Students are also prompted to draw the axes for a coordinate plane in the middle of the foldable. Finally, Ms. Fernandez makes sure each student is using a different-colored writing utensil from other members in their groups, as this will help with tracking individual progress and accountability. She provides colored pencils to help with this and instructs students as follows:

> You will be working on four total problems with your groups. Each of you will work on the same part of a different problem at the same time. For example, during the first round, everyone will be identifying the slope and y-intercept from an equation and using that information to graph the line in the middle of the foldable. Each paper needs to be labeled as either Problem 1, Problem 2, Problem 3, or Problem 4. Please decide which is which at your group now.

Ms. Fernandez uses this pause in instructions to make sure students are getting properly organized and that each group has only one of each labeled problem. She welcomes her students' attention back to her and continues, "Remember students, our social learning intention is to transition smoothly between roles during conversation roundtable. This is a process we're still learning about so paying close attention to the directions will help you be successful."

Satisfied with the level of attention she has from her students, Ms. Fernandez continues:

> So after the first round, where we will all be graphing lines from slope-intercept equations, I will instruct you to pass your paper to the group member to your left. Once we have rotated papers, we will start the second round, and I will project four different equations in standard form. You'll rewrite them into slope-intercept form and use that to graph them. After you have all had a chance to graph your own equations, we will pass again (to the left), and I'll project further instructions about approximating solutions. Each step of the task will be individual until the end when we do our error analyses together. Are there any questions about the general flow of this task?

EFFECT SIZE FOR COOPERATIVE LEARNING = 0.40

Ms. Fernandez answers questions and allows students to present a few hypotheticals, just to make sure they truly understand the expectations of the protocol. Once she is confident that they have the gist, she begins by projecting the first four equations. Students work through this protocol as Ms. Fernandez scans the room and notes how each group is progressing.

Two of the four problems in this task align with student expectations in that they have similar results to the prior in-class examples—a single solution each. The other two, however, are curveballs meant to spur collaborative conversations during the final error-analysis phase. One problem has no solutions because the two provided equations result in parallel lines that never intersect. The other curveball problem results in the same graph for each equation and thus has infinitely many solutions. Ms. Fernandez likes introducing special cases in collaborative spaces like this so that students have yet another opportunity to engage in transfer within mathematics. As she sees it, they arguably already possess the tools to make sense of these special cases on their own, so she wants to provide them that opportunity. Sure enough, as the task proceeds she begins hearing the telltale gasps of students being sent into disequilibrium from their results. She even hears a few exasperated, "What?! They can't do *that*!" types of comments. *It worked*, she thinks to herself. She'll use these perturbations as a bridge toward new conceptual understanding.

Teaching for Clarity at the Close

Ms. Fernandez closes class with a discussion centered on those unexpected curveball cases. She designs her questions to elicit comparing and contrasting of expected and unexpected cases, how to express the solutions (or lack thereof) of these new cases, and what might cause these results. Thus, Ms. Fernandez demonstrates the often cyclic relationship between procedural knowledge and conceptual understanding. She used conceptual understanding as the driver for teaching procedural knowledge, which in turn became the driver for additional conceptual understanding. Figure 4.7 shows how Ms. Fernandez made her planning visible so that she could then provide an engaging and rigorous learning experience for her learners.

Ms. Fernandez's Teaching for Clarity PLANNING GUIDE

ESTABLISHING PURPOSE

1   **What are the key content standards I will focus on in this lesson?**

Content Standards:

8.EE.C.8

    Analyze and solve pairs of simultaneous linear equations.

    b. . . . Estimate solutions [of a system] by graphing the equations.

Standards for Mathematical Practice:

- Make sense of problems and persevere in solving them.
- Use appropriate tools strategically.
- Reason abstractly and quantitatively.

2   **What are the learning intentions (the goal and *why* of learning stated in student-friendly language) I will focus on in this lesson?**

Content: I am learning to use our understanding of graphing linear functions as a means of solving systems of equations.

Language: I am learning to communicate the solutions to systems of equations verbally and in writing.

Social: I am learning to transition smoothly between roles during conversation roundtable.

3   **When will I introduce and reinforce the learning intention(s) so that students understand it, see the relevance, connect it to previous learning, and can clearly communicate it themselves?**

After introducing the learning intentions at the beginning of class, I will rely heavily on the social intention to facilitate the task of the day. I will also explicitly readdress the content and language intentions during direct/deliberate instruction as I model their intent.

SUCCESS CRITERIA

4 What evidence shows that students have mastered the learning intention(s)? What criteria will I use?

I can statements:

- *I can (still) graph linear equations.*
- *I can approximate solutions to systems of equations by creating graphs.*
- *I can explain solutions to systems of equations in writing.*

5 How will I check students' understanding (assess learning) during instruction and make accommodations?

In addition to providing space throughout direct/deliberate instruction for questions, I will monitor the room through the guided practice phase and sit with students who need extra support. I will also collect the conversation roundtable foldables as exit tickets for formative data.

INSTRUCTION

6 What activities and tasks will move students forward in their learning?

Focused Instruction

Students will take notes on graphing systems and approximating their solutions.

Guided Practice

Students will work through an example problem similar to their notes. I will scan the room and sit with students who need more support. Students will explain their methods and solutions at the board.

Collaborative Learning

We will do a collaborative activity involving a conversation roundtable foldable on graph paper. In groups of four, students will work in rounds completing four separate problems. During the first round, each group member will be graphing a linear function presented in slope-intercept form on their assigned problem. Once time is up, students will pass their foldable to their left and receive a new foldable from their right. During the second round, each group member will now graph an additional linear function presented in point-slope form on their newly received foldables. After passing again and now receiving a third foldable, they will approximate the solution to the system that should be graphed before them. On the fourth and final round, students will explain the solution provided from round 3 in writing. At the end of this process, the students will have four completed problems. Solutions will be posted for each and students will conduct an error analysis of their work. Additionally, two of these systems will be unlike the cases discussed in class and will spur a whole-class conversation.

Independent Learning

Students will have a short homework assignment aligned to each success criterion.

7 **What resources (materials and sentence frames) are needed?**

1. Graph paper for conversation roundtable foldables
2. Colored pencils or pens for foldables (different color for each group member)

8 **How will I organize and facilitate the learning? What questions will I ask? How will I initiate closure?**

This lesson will be an almost-linear path through the gradual release of responsibility. I will begin with focused instruction, then transition to guided practice, and then we will start our collaborative task. After the collaborative task, we will close with a whole-class discussion and students will be assigned an independent learning homework assignment aligned to today's success criteria.

 This lesson plan is available for download at resources.corwin.com/vlmathematics-6-8.

Figure 4.7   Ms. Fernandez's Procedural Lesson on Systems of Linear Equations

Mr. Singh and Integers

Mr. Singh knows that his students must build their fluency with integer operations both to meet the grade-level standards and because they provide a solid foundation for success in algebra. While fluency is often interpreted as meaning *fast and accurate*, Mr. Singh believes in a more nuanced definition. His state's curriculum framework defines computational, or procedural, fluency this way:

> Computational fluency refers to having flexible, efficient, and accurate methods for computing. Students exhibit computational fluency when they demonstrate strategic thinking and flexibility in the computational methods they choose, understand and can explain, and produce accurate answers efficiently. (Virginia Department of Education, 2016, p. v)

What Mr. Singh Wants His Students to Learn

In order to address fluency in this rich way, Mr. Singh has decided to spend several days taking his students through a series of experiences around integer addition and subtraction. This first lesson focuses on one structure of addition, the active "adding to" situation we think about when we consider contexts in which a situation changes when something arrives. In primary grades, this includes animals coming into an enclosure, students joining a classroom, baking cookies, earning money, and other similar settings. Mr. Singh will return to these familiar

---

MATHEMATICS CONTENT AND PRACTICE STANDARDS

Virginia Mathematics Standards of Learning 6.6

The student will

a. add, subtract, multiply, and divide integers.

Mr. Singh is helping his learners develop the following Mathematical Process Goal for Students:

• Mathematical problem solving

EFFECT SIZE
FOR STRATEGY
MONITORING = 0.58

situations (along with others more appropriate for middle school learners) as he helps his students develop conjectures about the rules which support integer addition. In future lessons, students will explore active subtraction situations (spending money or losing something) and then move into part-part-whole and comparison situations in which the inverse relationship between addition and subtraction is more evident.

By the end of the series, Mr. Singh plans for his students to have a variety of strategies and representations they can use to solve and explain integer addition and subtraction.

Mr. Singh's students must learn about all four operations with integers. He will begin with focusing solely on addition, however, because this experience lays the foundation for the idea of zero pairs (an essential concept for making sense of integer operation procedures). His specific learning intentions focus on these critical elements of the standards.

Learning Intentions and Success Criteria

MARGINAL EFFECT
SIZE = EFFECT
SIZE FOR PEER
TUTORING = 0.53

MARGINAL EFFECT
SIZE: EFFECT SIZE
FOR ASSESSMENT-
CAPABLE VISIBLE
LEARNERS = 1.33

Mr. Singh's social learning intention for the day includes the use of peer consultants. The class is learning about this practice, in which students who are confident in their thinking can serve as consultants to their classmates who might still be struggling. These peer consultants help their classmates by asking questions and engaging in discussion. The core rule is that consultants may not use a writing implement. Mr. Singh follows this same rule in his own practice because he has noticed that if he holds a pencil, he is more likely to write on the students' papers and do the thinking for them.

Content Learning Intention: I am learning to understand how to add integers, including seeing connections to active whole number addition and finding patterns to develop rules.

Language Learning Intention: I am learning to use language such as *distance, amount of change, positive, negative, addition, zero pair,* and *equals* precisely in describing their work.

Social Learning Intention: I am learning to work independently and use peer consultants when needed.

The success criteria make clear that this lesson focuses on procedures for adding integers. Students know from the beginning that they are expected to find correct solutions, to use manipulative tools to support this process, and to explain why methods work even when solving without the models.

> ☐ I can correctly solve addition of integers problems using number lines or counters.
>
> ☐ I can explain why the methods work when I solve without using a physical or visual model.

Modeling Strategies and Skills

Mr. Singh tells the class they will be working individually on word problems about adding integers today. They can use number lines or counters to support their thinking. He takes the class through an example to begin the lesson.

> Susan has $10 saved from doing chores around the house. She also owes a friend $3 because she forgot to take money for a snack to the fair. What is Susan's net worth?

Mr. Singh asks a student to read the problem aloud and then to describe the situation.

"Mr. Singh," one student wonders aloud. "What's *net worth*?"

"Ooh! Ooh!" Another student jolts his hand up, audibly emphasizing his wish to be called on to share his thinking. *If a student is that excited to talk about net worth*, Mr. Singh thinks to himself, *then I am definitely not going to stop him.* He gestures for the eager student to answer.

"It means add up what you have and what you owe!"

"Interesting," Mr. Singh says in a careful, nondescript tone as to not project the bias of his own endorsement of the student's response. "Do we agree or disagree with this definition and why? Please turn to your table partners and discuss for 30 seconds."

The student has offered a good definition for this lesson, and Mr. Singh uses it to continue the modeling process. "How can we represent Susan's $10 saved? What value is that?" Students name the value as positive 10 and represent it using 10 counters with the yellow side up or by marking positive 10 on the number line. They use open circles to sketch the yellow counters.

Mr. Singh knows that his elementary colleagues talk about these problems in terms of actions and a narrative so he asks what happens next. "Now what could we do to show the next part of the story?" Students agree that the $3 owed to a friend is a debt so would be represented by −3. With counters, this is easy: add three red counters to the model. There is more discussion about how to represent the negative three on the number line. Mr. Singh asks how they would represent the number when starting from zero and students show an arc moving three steps left. "Where are you starting now? Is it zero?" Students stop to think and one says, "No, we're starting at positive 10 this time." Mr. Singh sketches the arrow going three steps left to show negative three (Figure 4.8).

ADDING TEN AND NEGATIVE THREE

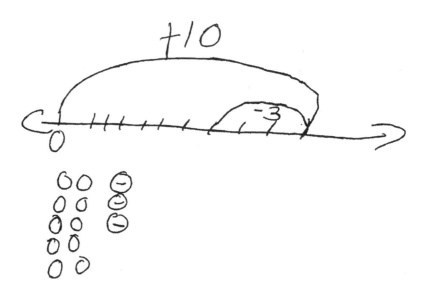

Figure 4.8

Mr. Singh asks the class what this tells them about Susan's net worth, the sum of what they have and what they owe. Students quickly see that the number line's story (following the arrows starting from zero) ends at positive seven. The counter model is more difficult. Students see 13 counters, yet they know the solution is not 13—in part, because some of the counters are red and some are yellow.

Pointing to the number line, Mr. Singh asks students what happens if they move positive one step and then negative one step. "We end up in the same place," they say. Mr. Singh asks what number we add to end up in the same place. The class calls out "zero" in chorus and Mr. Singh asks them to turn to a shoulder partner and see if they can find zero in the counters model. "What does it look like with counters when we take one step forward and one step back?"

> EFFECT SIZE FOR
> EVALUATION AND
> REFLECTION = 0.75

As they talk, students realize that a pair of counters, one red and one not red, show a value of zero because they model the pair of one step in each direction. Mr. Singh asks a student to explain his thinking about where the solution of positive seven is found in the counters model. The student says,

> I can pair these counters up (pointing to one red and one yellow) and that makes zero. I can do that three times with these three red ones from the debt. That's like paying back the debt. There are seven yellow counters left after I match these up so that's her $7 net worth.

Mr. Singh asks the class if anyone used a different way of pairing up the counters. Some pulled the pairs off to the side, while others stacked them on top of each other. Some worked pair by pair, while others looked at the group of three. Mr. Singh tells the class that these pairs of counters are called "zero pairs" and asks students to explain to a partner why this is an appropriate name. Listening to the discussions, he is comfortable asking students to proceed.

Instructional Approaches That Promote Procedural Fluency

Mr. Singh had decided to ask students to work individually on today's problems. This lesson builds on concepts students began to learn about in the primary grades, now incorporating both positive and negative

EFFECT SIZE
FOR DELIBERATE
PRACTICE = 0.79

EFFECT
SIZE FOR HELP
SEEKING = 0.72

numbers. The students have worked collaboratively to model situations with integers, and addition is the new step today. By asking students to work individually, Mr. Singh can see how well each student is making the connections from earlier study of addition. They will have peer support using each other as classroom consultants. As the students work, this routine helps keep the lesson moving because students are not always waiting for Mr. Singh for help. There is a classroom expectation that guides this peer support for learning:

- Ask for assistance, not the answer.
- Persevere in solving problems.
- Student consultants use their voices, not writing implements.

The rule of asking for assistance from peers first saves Mr. Singh from answering many of the detail questions that naturally come up in the course of a lesson ("Do we use red or yellow on the counters to represent negative numbers? How many problems are we supposed to do before we check our work with a partner?"). The reminder that consulting students use their voices rather than writing tools assures that consultants support rather than do the work for a classmate by writing on someone else's paper. Because Mr. Singh wants his students to work individually, he knows there might be many questions and these strategies allow him to focus on helping students with the mathematics of the lesson rather than filling in details. Now, it should be noted that Mr. Singh is well aware of the fact that he teaches sixth grade and that this first year in middle school can be a difficult social transition for some students. In an effort to foster positive student-teacher relationships and ensure that no one protocol or strategy is held in higher esteem than *every* student's learning, Mr. Singh breaks his own rules. For students that he has witnessed clam up rather than ask peers for assistance, Mr. Singh makes a point of checking in with them early in the day. Sometimes he will even say things like "With you, it can be me before others," which typically elicits a smile and an undercover high five. This little boost of confidence and support usually results in students willing to ask others for assistance.

Mr. Singh distributes a set of problems similar to the one the class has discussed and asks students to work independently to solve them. He instructs students to represent each addition problem using two-color counters or a number line and write an equation to summarize the mathematics of each problem, including the solution.

1. The temperature was –3 degrees Celsius when Mary woke up in the morning. While she was in school, the temperature increased 8 degrees. What was the temperature when Mary left school?

2. The football team gained 10 yards during the first play of the game and lost 4 yards in the second play of the game. What was their change in position after these first two plays?

Mr. Singh watches and listens as students begin to work. As expected, students are confident in building models for the situations. They are less confident in explaining how the models, especially with counters, show the solution. The use of consultants allows students to hear multiple perspectives on this explanation and practice giving explanations as well as receiving them.

Teaching for Clarity at the Close

After giving students time to work through the practice problems, Mr. Singh brings the class back together. He has already asked several students to share their models and thinking about the problems with the class, and they share their work in the sequence Mr. Singh planned. As the students question each other during sharing time, Mr. Singh is pleased to notice that they are asking one another clarifying questions about their work. Supporting his learners in asking each other clarifying questions has been the focus of his mathematics teaching for quite some time. He has devoted time to modeling this type of questioning so that learners could mimic this practice and eventually ask clarifying questions of one another.

Mr. Singh writes one more problem on the board. He asks the students to think about this one as mental math, first thinking about the equation and then about how they would solve it. Students work with a partner for this task.

Emma owes her brother $5. She earns $12 from her parents after helping with extra chores over the weekend. What is Emma's net worth?

As Mr. Singh listens to the discussions, he recognizes that students can write the equations for these situations comfortably, seeing this one as –5 + 12. He's listening for the strategies the students use to find their answers.

Video 13
Supporting Learners'
Extension to Transfer

*https://resources.corwin.com/
vlmathematics-6-8*

- Some students talk about imagining the counters and making zero pairs.

- Other students picture moving back and forth on the number line.

- When he hears a student talk about subtracting 5 from 12, Mr. Singh pauses. He listens a bit more and asks the student to share her thinking with the class in a moment.

STUDENT'S WORK FOR SOLVING THE PROBLEM USING A NUMBER LINE

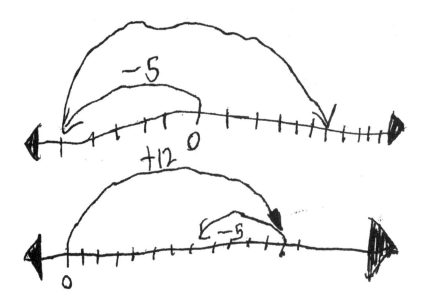

Figure 4.9

Bringing the class back together, Mr. Singh asks the student to share her strategy for solving this problem mentally. She says, "I pictured the problem on the number line and I realized that the part I need is the part that's left after I subtract 5 from 12. I drew this picture for 12 – 5 and it gives me the same answer" (Figure 4.9).

Mr. Singh asks the class if they think this strategy will work every time. As class ends, they agree to continue the discussion tomorrow because they are not sure.

Mr. Singh is pleased with the progress his students made. They are comfortable with adding integers using the strategies he has provided and are able to talk about the strategies they use. He's pleased that one student saw the subtraction connection as an answer-getting strategy in the final problem, and he considers how to incorporate that into the next day's lesson on subtraction. It might need to wait a day. He'll start subtraction with problems where the signs are the same and build to problems that require zero pairs to subtract when signs are not alike. He will circle back to today's closing conjecture when he wants students to see that there is more than one computation giving the same result: $-5 + 12 = 12 - (+5) = 12 + (-5) = 7$. Although each of these expressions represents a different real-world situation, they are computationally equivalent and any one can be used to find the answer to a question. Figure 4.10 shows how Mr. Singh made his planning visible so that he could then provide an engaging and rigorous learning experience for his learners.

Mr. Singh's Teaching for Clarity PLANNING GUIDE

ESTABLISHING PURPOSE

1 What are the key content standards I will focus on in this lesson?

Content Standards:

Virginia Mathematics Standards of Learning 6.6

The student will

a. add, subtract, multiply, and divide integers.

Mathematical Process Goal for Students:

- Mathematical problem solving

2 What are the learning intentions (the goal and *why* of learning stated in student-friendly language) I will focus on in this lesson?

Content: I am learning to understand how to add integers, including seeing connections to active whole number addition and finding patterns to develop rules.

Language: I am learning to use language such as *distance, amount of change, positive, negative, addition, zero pair,* and *equals* precisely in describing their work.

Social: I am learning to work independently and use peer consultants when needed.

3 When will I introduce and reinforce the learning intention(s) so that students understand it, see the relevance, connect it to previous learning, and can clearly communicate it themselves?

I will do this at the beginning of the lesson in order to set the stage.

SUCCESS CRITERIA

4

What evidence shows that students have mastered the learning intention(s)? What criteria will I use?

I can statements:

- I can correctly solve addition of integers problems using number lines or counters.
- I can explain why the methods work when I solve without using a physical or visual model.

5

How will I check students' understanding (assess learning) during instruction and make accommodations?

I will spot-check for correct solutions. I will listen to student explanations (to partners and to me). For students who struggle, I will provide additional models and examples, including explanations from peers who are finding success.

INSTRUCTION

6

What activities and tasks will move students forward in their learning?

Students will use chips or a number line to model simple whole number addition problems given a single situation with multiple values inserted. As students work with the problems, they will look for patterns that will help them find the solution using mental math.

7 What resources (materials and sentence frames) are needed?

Number lines, two-color counters, word problems

8 How will I organize and facilitate the learning? What questions will I ask? How will I initiate closure?

Students will solve simple problems using reasoning and modeling while looking for patterns. While working independently, students will use peer consultants to help them with their thinking. Class examples will focus on active addition (adding to) using both number lines and counters. After students identify patterns (rules) that generalize, they will begin to practice integer addition.

 This lesson plan is available for download at resources.corwin.com/vlmathematics-6-8.

Figure 4.10   Mr. Singh's Procedural Lesson on Integers

Reflection

Our final visit to these three classrooms focused on the development of procedural knowledge and fluency. Using what you have read in this chapter, reflect on the following questions:

1. In your own words, describe what teaching for procedural knowledge looks like in your mathematics classroom.

2. How does the Teaching for Clarity Planning Guide support your intentionality in teaching for procedural knowledge?

3. Compare and contrast the approaches to teaching taken by the classroom teachers featured in this chapter.

4. Consider the following statement: *Procedural knowledge is more than "drill and kill."* Do you agree or disagree with the statement? Why or why not? How is this statement reflected in this chapter?

5. How did the classroom teachers featured in this chapter adjust the difficulty and/or complexity of the mathematics tasks to meet the needs of all learners?

KNOWING YOUR IMPACT: EVALUATING FOR MASTERY

5

CHAPTER 5 SUCCESS CRITERIA:

(1) I can describe what mastery learning is in my classroom.

(2) I can compare and contrast checks for understanding with the evaluation of mastery.

(3) I can explain how to evaluate mastery in my own classroom using tasks and tests.

(4) I can identify characteristics of challenging mathematics tasks.

(5) I can explain the role of feedback in supporting students' journey to mastery.

Let us end right where we began—Ms. Norris's seventh grade mathematics classroom. Ms. Norris established a clear learning intention and success criteria, and she designed a challenging mathematics task that allowed learners to see themselves as their own teachers. Just like Ms. Halstrom, Ms. Fernandez, and Mr. Singh, Ms. Norris created many opportunities for learners to make their thinking visible through her checks for understanding. Formative evaluation and feedback are critical components to teaching mathematics in the Visible Learning classroom.

> EFFECT SIZE
> FOR PROVIDING
> FORMATIVE
> EVALUATION = 0.48
> AND FEEDBACK
> = 0.70

However, this chapter focuses on determining students' learning over the long haul. In other words, how do teachers assess for mastery? And in doing so, how do teachers and learners make evidence-informed decisions about when to move forward in the learning progression? Knowing our impact on student learning in mathematics involves more than just formative evaluation of learning. Knowing our impact also involves recognizing student mastery in their mathematics learning.

What Is Mastery Learning?

> **Mastery learning** is the expectation that learners will grasp specific conceptual understanding, procedural knowledge, and the application of specific concepts and thinking skills.

Mastery learning is the expectation that learners will grasp specific conceptual understanding, procedural knowledge, and the application of specific concepts and thinking skills. This requires that teachers establish clarity about the learning in mathematics classrooms and then organize a series of logical experiences, noticing which students do and don't learn along the way. When students experience lesson clarity, they progress toward mastery. The claim underlying mastery learning is that all children can learn when provided with clear explanations of what it means to "master" the material being taught. Although mastery learning does not speak to the time learners need to reach mastery, all students continuously receive evaluative feedback on their performance. Learners know where they are in their learning, where they are going, and what they can do to bridge the gap.

> EFFECT SIZE FOR
> MASTERY LEARNING
> = 0.57

> EFFECT SIZE FOR
> TEACHER CLARITY
> = 0.75

In true mastery learning, students do not progress to the next unit until they have mastered the previous one. But "moving on" could mean that learners move forward in the learning progression or that they are provided additional learning experiences at the surface, deep, or transfer level to address gaps in their learning if they are not yet able to demonstrate mastery. Ms. Norris notes,

To evaluate student mastery, I develop a rubric that describes each level of proficiency. For example, Levels 1 through 4, with 4 being mastery. My feedback depends on the specific descriptions of each level. When learners demonstrate, say, a Level 1 or Level 2, I use this information to provide additional scaffolding for these learners. They are not there, *yet*.

Mastery learning is an essential part of building assessment-capable visible learners in the mathematics classroom. If learners are to know where they are going next in their learning, select the right learning tools to support the next steps tools (e.g., manipulatives, problem-solving approaches, and/or meta-cognitive strategies), and know what feedback to seek about their own learning, they must have opportunities to assess their own mastery with mathematics content. This, of course, comes after learners have engaged in multiple mathematics tasks replete with checks for understanding that allow teachers and students to adjust learning in the moment. Once that has occurred, it is time to determine students' level of mastery in the mathematics learning. So how do we determine what mastery looks like for specific content in the mathematics classroom?

Using Learning Intentions to Define Mastery Learning

Learning intentions provide the framework for defining mastery, developing the assessments used to determine student mastery, and gathering the information necessary to plan learning experiences for students. Ms. Norris, Ms. Halstrom, Ms. Fernandez, and Mr. Singh had to answer the question "What do my students need to learn?" The answer to this question represents mastery for the specific content in each of their classrooms. In the above example from Ms. Norris's classroom, the learning intention stated *I am learning that the unit rate dictates the slope of the line and that different proportional relationships can be represented in different ways*. Therefore, to demonstrate mastery, her learners must model and represent different proportional relationships.

Assessments of mastery require both the teacher and the learners to focus on the essential learning for a particular unit or series of lessons. Teachers must unpack the language of the specific standard to have a

---

Teaching Takeaway

Effective feedback is an essential feature of the Visible Learning mathematics classroom.

Teaching Takeaway

Features of mastery learning include the following:

1. Clear learning expectations
2. Feedback that is specific, constructive, and timely
3. Sufficient time, attention, and support to ensure learning

clear sense of the conceptual understanding, procedural knowledge, and applications expected in the mastery of the standard. Let us look at another example by first considering the following cluster of content standards:

> Analyze proportional relationships and use them to solve real-world and mathematical problems.

As you can see, this is not very helpful in developing and implementing an assessment of mastery learning. To narrow in on tasks that will allow students to demonstrate mastery, teachers must specifically define what the learner will know, understand, and be able to do. Ms. Norris and her collaborative planning team defined *mastery* as follows:

> I can analyze a real-world situation, describe the situation as a percent increase or percent decrease scenario, determine the values needed to calculate percent change, and perform the calculations.

In addition, Ms. Norris and her colleagues have specifically identified vocabulary that represents key concepts within this standard that learners must use fluently in their work: *percent, increase, decrease, percent change, percent increase,* and *percent decrease* (Figure 5.1).

Establishing the Expected Level of Mastery

From this preestablished level of mastery, which is based on the standard(s), teachers identify indicators that students are or are not at the level of mastery. These indicators should focus on what students are doing rather than what they are not doing. This helps identify current performance levels and is suggestive of the types of experiences students need to have to progress in their learning. In other words, what does progress toward mastery look like in this specific standard? Learners progress toward mastery at different rates, and teachers should map out that progress so that both the teacher and the learners can make an informed decision about where they are in their learning.

Ms. Norris and her colleagues identified the incremental steps along the pathway to achieving mastery for the functional relationship standard

EXAMPLE OF PROGRESS TOWARD MASTERY FOR A SPECIFIC CONTENT STANDARD

Content Standard: Analyze proportional relationships and use them to solve real-world and mathematical problems.	Learning Intention: I am learning to compute percent change for real-world situations.					Vocabulary
	How will I know when I have it? The following mastery levels will let you know how you are progressing toward this learning goal.					percent change percent increase percent decrease
	Level 4	Level 3	Level 2	Level 1	Level 0	**Prior Knowledge**
	I can read a real-world situation, determine the values needed to calculate percent change, and perform the calculations. I can describe the situation as a percent increase or a percent decrease.	Given a real-world situation, I can calculate the percent change for the situation. I may struggle with some computation or describing the situation as a percent increase or a percent decrease.	Given the old and new values, I can calculate the percent change and can describe the change as an increase or decrease.	I know the formula for percent change. Given the old and new values, I struggle to put the values into the formula correctly and/or I make computation errors.	I do not show an understanding of the concept of percent change.	percent increase or decrease

Source: Ashley Norris, Mathematics Teacher, Columbia County Public Schools, Georgia

Figure 5.1

 This rubric is available for download at resources.corwin.com/vlmathematics-6-8.

using the SOLO Taxonomy (see Figure 1.5 in Chapter 1). If students perceive themselves to be or actually are far from meeting the highest level of proficiency, making the progression visible allows them to answer the questions "Where am I going, how am I going, and where will I go next?" These are essential in developing assessment-capable visible learners. Ms. Halstrom, Ms. Fernandez, and Mr. Singh narrowed in on tasks that will allow students to demonstrate mastery; teachers must specifically define what the learner will know, understand, and be able to do (Figure 5.2).

DESCRIPTION OF MASTERY FOR MATHEMATICS CONTENT STANDARDS

	Mathematics Content Standard	What Mastery Looks Like
Ms. Halstrom	**From Chapter 4:** Solve real-life and mathematical problems involving angle measure, area, surface area, and volume. Know the formulas for the area and circumference of a circle and use them to solve problems; give an informal derivation of the relationship between the circumference and area of a circle.	Learners must explain the relationship between circumference and area of a circle. Then learners must use the formula to calculate the area of circles.
Ms. Fernandez	**From Chapter 3:** 8. Analyze and solve pairs of simultaneous linear equations. a. Understand that solutions to a system of two linear equations in two variables correspond to points of intersection of their graphs because points of intersection satisfy both equations simultaneously.	Given an authentic scenario (e.g., best recreational vehicle rental plan on a vacation), learners must model the scenario using a system of linear equations, calculate a solution, and interpret the mathematical results in the context of the scenario.
Mr. Singh	**From Chapter 2:** The student will a. add, subtract, multiply, and divide integers; and b. solve practical problems involving operations with integers.	Given an authentic scenario (e.g., temperature change, balancing a checking account, athletics, and/or changes in altitude), learners must model the scenario (e.g., using a number line, counters, drawings, or algebra tiles), calculate a solution, and interpret the mathematical results in the context of the scenario.

Figure 5.2

When we revisit the classrooms of Ms. Halstrom, Ms. Fernandez, and Mr. Singh, we see that they provide similar levels of clarity about what mastery looks like (see Figure 5.3). Teachers know their students best and therefore can use evaluation of student learning—within a set of learning intentions—to designate their students' levels of proficiency on the pathway to mastery. That said, there is no prescribed number of these levels.

	Mathematics Content Standard	Levels of Mastery
Ms. Halstrom	**From Chapter 4:** Solve real-life and mathematical problems involving angle measure, area, surface area, and volume. Know the formulas for the area and circumference of a circle and use them to solve problems; give an informal derivation of the relationship between the circumference and area of a circle. Apply properties of operations as strategies to add, subtract, factor, and expand linear expressions with rational coefficients.	**Level 1:** No clear explanation of the relationship between the circumference and area of the circle. Cannot substitute values into the formulae to calculate area and circumference. **Level 2:** Attempts to explain the relationship between the circumference and area of the circle. References key ideas but does not construct a clear argument. Struggles to use the formulae to calculate area and circumference. **Level 3:** Explains the relationship between circumference and area of the circle. Some vocabulary or descriptions may be imprecise. Uses the formulae correctly in calculating area and circumference with minor computational errors. **Level 4:** Clearly explains the relationship between circumference and area of the circle, using appropriate vocabulary and notation. Uses the formulae correctly in calculating area and circumference.
Ms. Fernandez	**From Chapter 3:** 8. Analyze and solve pairs of simultaneous linear equations. a. Understand that solutions to a system of two linear equations in two variables correspond to points of intersection of their graphs because points of intersection satisfy both equations simultaneously.	**Level 1:** Shows minimal attempt on the problem (guess and check); no clear problem-solving approach; no reasoning is provided with the answer; or no answer provided. **Level 2:** Shows signs of coherent problem solving; minimal evidence to support the answer; failed to address some of the constraints of the problem; occasionally makes sense of quantities in relationships in the problem; trouble generalizing or using the mathematical results. **Level 3:** Shows the main elements of solving the problem; an organized approach to solving the problem; there are errors, but of a kind that the student could well fix, with more time for checking and revision and some limited help; makes sense of quantities and their relationships in the specific situation; response uses assumptions, definitions, and previously established results.

(Continued)

(Continued)

	Mathematics Content Standard	Levels of Mastery
		Level 4: Shows understanding and use of stated assumptions, definitions, and previously established results in construction arguments; makes conjectures and builds a logical progression of statements; routinely interprets their mathematical results in the context of the situation and reflects on whether the results make sense; communication is precise, using definitions clearly.
Mr. Singh	**From Chapter 2:** The student will a. add, subtract, multiply, and divide integers; and b. solve practical problems involving operations with integers.	**Level 1:** Shows minimal attempt on the problem (guess and check); no clear problem-solving approach; no reasoning is provided with the answer; or no answer provided. **Level 2:** Shows signs of coherent problem solving; minimal evidence to support the answer; failed to address some of the constraints of the problem; occasionally makes sense of quantities in relationships in the problem; trouble generalizing or using the mathematical results. **Level 3:** Shows the main elements of solving the problem; an organized approach to solving the problem; there are errors, but of a kind that the student could well fix, with more time for checking and revision and some limited help; makes sense of quantities and their relationships in the specific situation; response uses assumptions, definitions, and previously established results. **Level 4:** Shows understanding and use of stated assumptions, definitions, and previously established results in construction arguments; makes conjectures and builds a logical progression of statements; routinely interprets their mathematical results in the context of the situation and reflects on whether the results make sense; communication is precise, using definitions clearly.

Figure 5.3

Collecting Evidence of Progress Toward Mastery

To determine progress and to support the grades given to students, teachers must be able to clearly answer the question "What evidence suggests that the learners have mastered the learning, or are moving toward mastery?" The evidence used to determine mastery is typically

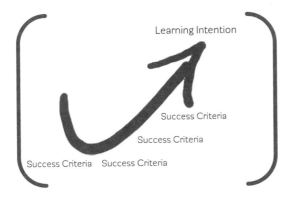

Learning Intention

Success Criteria

Success Criteria

Success Criteria   Success Criteria

Checks for Understanding gather and provide *evidence of learners' progress* toward a learning intention using the success criteria as guides for this progression.

Figure 5.4

more formal than the evidence used to check for understanding. For example, an exit ticket could easily be used to determine which students mastered a given learning intention on a given day. But that may not be sufficient evidence for determining mastery of a standard or set of standards. Checks for understanding gather and provide *evidence of a learner's progress* toward a learning intention, whereas an evaluation of mastery provides *evidence that a student has demonstrated mastery* of a standard or set of standards.

The difference between checks for understanding and evaluating for mastery lies in the focus of the task, as well as the use of the evidence. In a check for understanding, teachers and students are gathering evidence about learning around specific learning intentions and success criteria (see Figure 5.4).

Ms. Halstrom, Ms. Fernandez, and Mr. Singh had multiple checks for understanding throughout their lessons. In each of their classrooms, learners engaged in checks for understanding that targeted the specific learning intentions and success criteria for the lesson.

Although we can use formative assessments collected over time to evaluate mastery—evidence over time—our classrooms require single

Teaching Takeaway

In addition to knowing what we want our students to learn, we have to know what evidence will demonstrate that they have learned it.

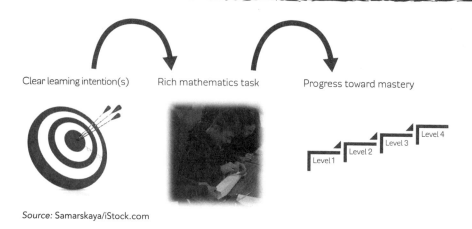

Clear learning intention(s)   Rich mathematics task   Progress toward mastery

Level 1   Level 2   Level 3   Level 4

Source: Samarskaya/iStock.com

Figure 5.5

tasks that evaluate mastery (e.g., performance-based learning tasks and well-designed standardized tests). These tasks evaluate student mastery by focusing on the standard(s), asking learners to assimilate all of the learning into *a challenging mathematics task* (sometimes called a *rich mathematical task*). Again, evaluating student mastery brings together multiple concepts, procedures, and applications into a single task rather than rich tasks that target specific success criteria within a standard or standards. These tasks can include, but are not limited to, performance-based learning tasks and well-designed standardized tests (see Figure 5.5).

Figure 5.6 includes a checklist useful in creating assessment of mastery. As Ms. Norris says,

> After our team develops an assessment for mastery, we use the checklist to make sure that it's the best assessment we can develop. We don't want false positives or false negatives, meaning data that suggest students are mastering content when they are not or students who need more learning but look like they have mastered it based on the assessment.

CHECKLIST FOR CREATING OR SELECTING TASKS THAT ASSESS MASTERY

All Items

❏ Is this the most appropriate type of item to use for the intended learning outcomes?

❏ Does each item or task require students to demonstrate the performance described in the specific learning outcome it measures (relevance)?

❏ Does each item present a clear and definite task to be performed (clarity)?

❏ Is each item or task presented in simple, readable language and free from excessive verbiage (conciseness)?

❏ Does each item provide an appropriate challenge (ideal difficulty)?

❏ Does each item have an answer that would be agreed upon by experts (correctness)?

❏ Is there a clear basis for awarding partial credit on items or tasks with multiple points (scoring rubric)?

❏ Is each item or task free from technical errors and irrelevant clues (technical soundness)?

❏ Is each test item free from cultural bias?

❏ Have the items been set aside for a time before reviewing them (or being reviewed by a colleague)?

Performance Items

❏ Does the item focus on learning outcomes that require complex cognitive skills and student performances?

❏ Does the task represent both the content and skills that are central to learning outcomes?

❏ Does the item minimize dependence on skills that are irrelevant to the intended purpose of the assessment task?

❏ Does the task provide the necessary scaffolding for students to be able to understand the task and achieve the task?

❏ Do the directions clearly describe the task?

❏ Are students aware of the basis (expectations) on which their performances will be evaluated in terms of scoring rubrics?

Source: Adapted from Linn, R. L., & Gronlund, N. E. (2000). *Measurement and assessment in teaching* (8th ed.). Upper Saddle River, NJ: Merrill Prentice Hall.

Figure 5.6

 This checklist is available for download at resources.corwin.com/vlmathematics-6-8.

A poorly designed task washes out the benefit of determining learner mastery. For example, a group of teachers were looking to see if learners could compare proportional relationships represented multiple ways. The teachers developed a sorting and matching task, but that did not

> Poorly designed tasks yield poor evidence and poor decisions about where to go next.

> What separates a challenging, rich mathematics task from a rote exercise is the nature of the cognitive engagement required to complete the task.

provide them with the evidence needed to make a decision about student proficiency. We are not saying that a sorting or matching task never works; however, a sorting task at this time, for this content, will not provide the evidence needed to make a decision about student proficiency. Furthermore, if the task is not engaging and relevant to our students, their level of persistence will likely skew the evidence as well. Whether the evaluation of mastery provides evidence to the teacher and student about the current level of mastery is the nature of the task itself. In other words, poorly designed tasks yield poor evidence and poor decisions about where to go next.

In order to develop an effective evaluation that provides opportunities for learners to demonstrate mastery while at the same time provides evidence for feedback or next steps, teachers should consider the ways students can make their mathematics thinking visible. What separates a challenging, rich mathematics task from a rote exercise is the nature of the cognitive engagement required to complete the task. In mathematics exercises, learners repeat terms, concepts, ideas, procedures, or processes and apply those in novel situations.

Let us look at the set of mastery tasks developed by Ms. Norris and her team. How a learner approaches these tasks and the thinking these tasks generate provide valuable information to both the teacher and the learner, allowing learners to gain an understanding of where they are in their learning progression, identify where they need to go next in their learning, and what learning tools are needed to support this next step. What do we mean by *challenging, rich mathematics tasks*? There are many definitions:

- Accessible to all learners ("low floor, high ceiling")
- Real-life task or application
- Multiple approaches and representations
- Collaboration and discussion
- Engagement, curiosity, and creativity
- Making connections within and/or across topics and domains, vertically and horizontally
- Opportunities for extension (adapted from Boaler, 2015, 2016; Wolf, 2015)

These tasks are far different from forced-choice items that may only assess the guesswork of mathematics learners. Bringing the previous definitions to life, Antonetti and Garver (2015) reported on data from classroom walk-throughs that focused on eight features of classroom activities that differentiated mathematics tasks from mere rote exercises. Observers measured consistent and sustained engagement when three or more of the features were present. The eight characteristics of challenging mathematics tasks are as follows:

1. **Personal response:** Do students have the opportunity to bring their own personal experiences with mathematics to the task? Examples include any task that invites learners to bring their own background, interests, or expertise to the task. This might be an activity that provides learners with the option to create their own strategies and approaches, make connections to ideas important in their own lives, allow them to create their own representations, or let them select the context in which a concept is explored (e.g., selection of a specific book or creation of their own problem). These examples have one thing in common: They allow learners to personalize their responses to meet their background, interests, or expertise. As we evaluate mastery, insight into how learners are making meaning of the conceptual understanding, procedural knowledge, and application of concepts and thinking skills is important.

2. **Clear and modeled expectations:** Do learners have a clear understanding of what they are supposed to do in this mathematics task? This characteristic refers us back to clear learning intentions, success criteria, learning progressions, exemplars, models, worked examples, and rubrics. We will take an additional look at the role of rubrics later in this chapter. Do your learners know what success looks like in this task, or are they blindly hoping to hit the end target that you have in mind for them?

3. **Sense of audience:** Do learners have a sense that this mathematics work matters to someone other than the teacher and the gradebook? Tasks that have a sense of audience mean something to individuals beyond the teacher, which provides authenticity.

Sense of audience can be established by cooperative learning or group work in which individual members have specific roles, as in a jigsaw. Other examples include community-based projects or service projects that utilize mathematics and contribute to the local, school, or classroom community (e.g., analyzing data from a local stream).

4. **Social interaction:** Do learners have opportunities to socially interact with their peers? Providing learners with opportunities to talk about mathematics and interact with their peers supports their meaning making and development of conceptual understanding as well as the application of concepts and thinking skills. In addition, teachers and learners get to hear other students' mathematics thinking.

5. **Emotional safety:** Do learners feel safe in asking questions or making mistakes? Even though this task seeks to evaluate the level of mastery in mathematics content, learners must still believe that they will learn from mistakes and that errors are welcomed even at this stage of their learning. To be blunt, if learners feel threatened in your mathematics classroom, they will not engage in any mathematics task.

6. **Choice:** Do learners have choices in how they access the mathematics task? As learners engage with procedures, concepts, or their application, we should offer choices around who they work with, what materials and manipulatives are available, and what mathematics learning strategies they can use to accomplish the task. In addition, we should offer them multiple ways to show us what they know about the mathematics content.

7. **Novelty:** Does the task require learners to approach the mathematics from a unique perspective? Examples of this characteristic include engaging scenarios, discrepant events, scientific phenomena demonstrations, or games and puzzles.

8. **Authenticity:** Does the task represent an authentic learning experience, or is the experience sterile and unrealistic (e.g., a worksheet, problem-solving scenario)? We can offer learners a scenario around packaging and the volume of a rectangular

prism versus the volume of a cylinder. Learners would have to make a decision about the material needed to construct each package, the volume the package would hold, and the cost-effectiveness between the two packages (adapted from Schlechty, 2002).

To evaluate the level of mastery in mathematics learning, teachers must design and implement tasks that provide opportunities for learners to truly demonstrate what they know, how they know it, and why they know it.

Ensuring Tasks Evaluate Mastery

Ms. Norris is preparing to evaluate students' mastery in proportional relationships and how to use proportional reasoning to solve authentic problems (e.g., tips, tax, discounts, etc.). Specifically, Ms. Norris wants to know if her learners are ready to move on from percents of change to dilation transformations and similarity. Throughout the week, she has utilized checks for understanding to gather and provide evidence of her learners' progress in the following tasks:

Video 14
Evaluating for Mastery

*https://resources.corwin.com/
vlmathematics-6-8*

- Calculating percent of change

- Understanding percents greater than 100

- Describing multiplicative comparison situations and solving them correctly

- Naming geometric figures and identifying necessary elements of the figures

She aligned her checks for understanding with the success criteria and specific learning intentions for each lesson. Ms. Norris's checks for understanding allow her to evaluate her students' progress and adjust their learning experiences, but they do not allow her to determine mastery of the content. Mastery assessments are used more summatively, whereas checks for understanding are used more formatively. But know that assessments are neither formative nor summative by nature; it's all in the use of the tool. And as you will see, the mastery assessments are often used to guide future learning experiences for students. Thus, they are tools that include multiple learning intentions, are typically administered at the unit level, can be used as evidence of longer-term learning, and are often used as the basis for grades. Having said that, if we really believe in mastery, grades would be updated throughout the year as students demonstrate competency of previous content. Thus, the grades for a unit taught in October might be updated when students demonstrate deeper understanding in December. For more information on competency-based or standards-based grading, see Guskey (2014). To design or select a task or possibly a cohesive set of tasks for evaluating mastery, teachers should do the following:

1. Return to the learning intentions and success criteria associated with content for which we are evaluating mastery. What is it that students were supposed to learn?

2. Create a challenging mathematics task (or a set of tasks) that requires learners to demonstrate their proficiency for each specific learning intention and success criterion. In other words, can students do what each of the learning intentions says they should be able to do?

3. Identify criteria for mastery and levels of progress toward mastery.

For proportional relationships and how to use proportional reasoning to solve authentic problems, Ms. Norris asked her learners to engage in a series of tasks. She instructed her learners to complete as much of each task as possible, flagging areas where they need additional learning.

TASK 1

Given real-world data explicitly labeled as old and new values, calculate the percent change and describe it as an increase or decrease.

TASK 2

Students will be given real-world situations and perform close reading of those items. Using highlighters and other resources, students will learn to identify pertinent information, state what values are represented, and compute the percent change.

TASK 3

Research the number of households that owned a PlayStation 4 in 2014 and then in 2017. Compute the percent change in years and describe it as an increase or decrease. If you have an idea for other data you would like to research, present them to me for approval.

TASK 4

Research a real-world situation of your own choosing and calculate the percent change. Describe each change as an increase or a decrease.

Source: Ashley Norris, Mathematics Teacher, Columbia County Public Schools, Georgia

 These tasks are available for download at resources.corwin.com/vlmathematics-6-8.

She then used the team's progression toward mastery levels to evaluate mastery (see Figure 5.1).

Ensuring Tests Evaluate Mastery

Tasks are great, but there will always be mathematics tests. Tests not only are common in the mathematics classroom but can also be an effective means for determining the mastery of learners. The intention and design of any test determines the usefulness of the evidence generated about learner mastery. Whether multiple choice or open-ended, tests must provide the necessary evidence about student learning so that both the teacher and the learners can make a clear evaluation of their understanding with the specific mathematics content. In designing a mathematics test, we must take into account several aspects of that test if we are to achieve high-quality evaluation of student learning.

The first aspect of a well-designed test is that the test items align with the expectations of the standard and associated learning intentions and success criteria.

Whether in our own classroom or in the classrooms of the teachers featured in this book, the test designed to evaluate learner mastery must contain questions or items that are consistent with the teaching and learning in that classroom. If the focus in Ms. Halstrom's seventh grade classroom is on the memorization and execution of formulas (e.g., procedural knowledge in finding the area of a circle), then an end of unit or standard test cannot contain items that solely focus on conceptual understanding or application and provide a clear evaluation of student mastery (e.g., develop definitions of circles and their characteristics). Likewise, if the focus in Ms. Halstrom's seventh grade class is on the conceptual understanding of circles, parallelograms, and relationships between determining the area of a circle, a test for mastery cannot contain items that only focus on formulas.

Therefore, the first aspect of a well-designed test is that the test items align with the expectations of the standard and associated learning intentions and success criteria.

Test items should provide learners with the opportunity to demonstrate different levels of mastery. In addition to having test items that align with the expectations of the standard, a well-designed test will have questions that fall in the progression toward the standard. For example, in Ms. Fernandez's class, her students must be able to analyze and solve linear equations and pairs of simultaneous linear equations; they must also understand that solutions to a system of two linear equations in two variables correspond to points of intersection of their graphs, because points of intersection satisfy both equations simultaneously. That is the expectation of the standard. The test should include items that ask her learners to find the solution of a system of linear equations from graphs and mathematical calculations. In addition, the test might ask learners to explain how each approach allows them to locate the solution to a system of linear equations. Including the components that build up to the standard will allow Ms. Fernandez to determine how much learners have mastered if they have not fully mastered the standard.

Teaching Takeaway

There should be items on the test that build up to the standard or mastery level.

As we reflect back on our days as middle school mathematics students, we can likely recall instances where we missed questions on a test because we were not clear on what the question was asking us to do. When we received feedback on the test, we may have responded to that feedback with "Oh, that's what you wanted on number 15?"

Using consistent language on a test is vital in evaluating the learning of mathematics compared to semantics. As students engage in mathematics learning, we must ensure that the language we expect them to master is the language we use in the learning experiences. For example, if Mr. Singh plans to include questions on his test that use the term *zero pairs*, or *amount of change*, then this concept should be introduced during the learning experiences. Likewise, if he is going to reference the use of physical or visual models like number lines or counters for solving integer problems, learners need experiences with those tools. Using consistent language applies to the cognitive aspects of the questions as well. We must ensure learners know what we mean by *analyze*, *explain*, or *support your answer*.

Figure 5.7 provides additional guidelines for developing well-designed tests. These checklists help to ensure that our tests provide clear evidence about our learners' mastery in mathematics.

If our ultimate goal is for students to see themselves as their own mathematics teacher, we have to devote time to helping them prepare for tests. Simply telling our learners to "study" is not enough to support them in their journey to becoming assessment-capable visible learners in mathematics. As you can see, we have come full circle in this book. Ensuring that learners have clarity about the learning intentions, success criteria, and their progress toward those items will then help them prepare for this evaluation of mastery. Providing learners with opportunities to connect the learning intentions and success criteria to the type of question they will likely see on a test encourages them to take ownership of their mathematics learning.

Feedback for Mastery

With the learning intention clear, a definition of success established, and a challenging mathematics assessment of mastery developed and implemented, the nature of the feedback on learners' performance is an essential and necessary component in the Visible Learning mathematics classroom. Depending on the level of mastery demonstrated by the learner, specific, constructive, and timely feedback supports learners as they—together with the teacher—evaluate where they are going, how they are going, and where they are going next.

Teaching Takeaway

Students should be familiar with the language of the test.

Teaching Takeaway

We must help our learners understand what it means to study for a mathematics test.

Depending on the level of mastery demonstrated by the learner, specific, constructive, and timely feedback supports learners as they—together with the teacher—evaluate where they are going, how they are going, and where they are going next.

CHECKLISTS FOR CREATING TESTS THAT ASSESS MASTERY

Short-Answer Items

- ☐ Can the items be answered with a number, symbol, word, or brief phrase?
- ☐ Has textbook language been avoided?
- ☐ Have the items been stated so that only one response is correct?
- ☐ Are the answer blanks equal in length (for fill-in responses)?
- ☐ Are the answer blanks (preferably one per item) at the end of the items, preferably after a question?
- ☐ Are the items free of clues (such as *a* or *an*)?
- ☐ Has the degree of precision been indicated for numerical answers?
- ☐ Have the units been indicated when numerical answers are expressed in units?

Binary (True–False) and Multiple-Binary Items

- ☐ Can each statement be clearly judged true or false with only one concept per statement?
- ☐ Have specific determiners (e.g., usually, always) been avoided?
- ☐ Have trivial statements been avoided?
- ☐ Have negative statements (especially double negatives) been avoided?
- ☐ Does a superficial analysis suggest a wrong answer?
- ☐ Are opinion statements attributed to some source?
- ☐ Are the true and false items approximately equal in length?
- ☐ Is there approximately an equal number of true and false items?
- ☐ Has a detectable pattern of answers (e.g., *T, F, T, F*) been avoided?

Matching Items

- ☐ Is the material for the two lists homogeneous?
- ☐ Is the list of responses longer or shorter than the list of premises?
- ☐ Are the responses brief and on the right-hand side?
- ☐ Have the responses been placed in alphabetical or numerical order?
- ☐ Do the directions indicate the basis for matching?
- ☐ Do the directions indicate how many times each response may be used?
- ☐ Are all of the matching items on the same page?

Multiple-Choice Items
☐ Does each item stem present a meaningful problem?
☐ Is there too much information in the stem?
☐ Are the item stems free of irrelevant material?
☐ Are the item stems stated in positive terms (if possible)?
☐ If used, has negative wording been given special emphasis (e.g., capitalized)?
☐ Are the distractors brief and free of unnecessary words?
☐ Are the distractors similar in length and form to the answer?
☐ Is there only one correct or clearly best answer?
☐ Are the distractors based on specific misconceptions?
☐ Are the items free of clues that point to the answer?
☐ Are the distractors and answer presented in sensible (e.g., alphabetical, numerical) order?
☐ Has *all of the above* been avoided and *none of the above* used judiciously?
☐ If a stimulus is used, is it necessary for answering the item?
☐ If a stimulus is used, does it require use of skills sought to be assessed?

Source: Adapted from Linn, R. L., & Gronlund, N. E. (2000). *Measurement and assessment in teaching* (8th ed.). Upper Saddle River, NJ: Merrill Prentice Hall.

Figure 5.7

 This checklist is available for download at resources.corwin.com/vlmathematics-6-8.

Task Feedback

For learners at the earliest level of mastery, **task feedback** develops student understanding of specific procedures, concepts, and applications. This type of feedback is corrective, precise, and focused on the accuracy of the learners' responses to the mastery task. For example, Ms. Norris may provide written or verbal feedback that says, "Take a look at your calculation for Question 3. The ratio does not match your scenario or your ratio table." She may indicate to a learner that a specific question is wrong and needs revisiting before moving on in the learning.

> **Task feedback** addresses how well the task has been performed—correct or incorrect.

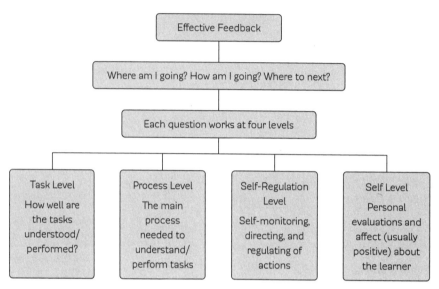

Source: Hattie & Timperley (2007).

Figure 5.8

On the other hand, she may say, "You identified the correct constant of proportionality. I really like how you checked your work by creating a ratio table. Now move on to calculation of the final price."

Learners rely on task feedback to add additional structure to their conceptual understanding, procedural knowledge, and application of concepts and thinking skills. This may include examples and non-examples, additional learning on procedural steps, and contexts of the task. Ms. Norris may sit down with a learner who has missed a specific question and provide additional examples for finding percent increase or decrease by focusing on benchmark percents like 10%, 25%, or 50%. She may even provide two scenarios and ask the learner to compare and contrast them to clarify understanding. Each learner's successful assimilation of feedback, and thus using the feedback to decide where to go next, rests solely on whether each learner understands what the feedback means and how he or she can use it to move forward with mathematics learning. Effective feedback (Figure 5.8) and effective use of that feedback support this initial learning.

Process Feedback

As learners begin to develop proficiency with specific content, ideas, and terms, the feedback should increasingly shift to process feedback. **Process feedback** is critical as learners explore the *why* and the *how* of specific mathematics content. In their initial assessment of mastery, learners received and assimilated task feedback into their work to develop a deeper understanding of procedures, concepts, and applications. To move learners beyond what is simply right or wrong, example or non-example, they must receive and incorporate feedback that focuses on the process or strategies associated with accomplishing the specific task. Returning to Ms. Norris's classroom, she may not indicate whether a particular response is correct or incorrect but she might simply ask, "Why do you believe that this is a percent increase? What information can you infer from the ratio table? Do you have any tools that would allow you to verify these assumptions?"

Whether from the teacher or peers, learners should receive feedback on their thinking, not just the accuracy of their response. For example, teachers might engage students in further dialogue about the use of specific strategies to solve a particular problem. Again, this feedback can come from the teacher or their peers. For example, Figure 5.9 shows an example of peer-assisted reflection (PAR) for solving systems by graphing in Ms. Fernandez's classroom (Reinholz, 2015). In this scenario, learners complete a draft solution—along with annotations explaining their thought process (not just *what* they did, by *why* they did it)—that is ready to be reviewed by a peer. The peer feedback is offered in two phases. First, peers provide each other written feedback in the form of annotations and a rating toward mastery of each success criterion during a silent review phase. Second, peers discuss the written feedback they provided and ask any clarifying questions they might have about that feedback. The final step for students is to revise their draft solution into a final submission and include a reflection of how their thinking changed throughout this process.

PEER-ASSISTED REFLECTION FOR SOLVING SYSTEMS BY GRAPHING

Solving Systems by Graphing

Name: Period: Date:

Write your solution in the left column. The right column is used for annotations. If you provide feedback to your peer, you will annotate their solution. After class, you will annotate your own solution as well. In your submission, use the annotation column to explain how you did (or didn't) respond to peer feedback.

Success Criteria

❑ I can (still) graph linear equations.

❑ I can approximate solutions to systems of equations by creating graphs.

❑ I can explain solutions to systems of equations in writing.

1) Graph the following linear equations on the same coordinate plane.

   a. $y = \frac{2}{3}x + 3$

   b. $y = 3x - 2$

   c. $y = -\frac{1}{2}x + 1$

2) Approximate the solution to the systems of equations made by

   a.   Equation A and Equation B

   b.   Equation A and Equation C

   c.   Equation B and Equation C

3) Explain in writing why your approximations represent the solution to each system of equations. How are you using your graphs to approximate each solution?

Reviewed by: _____

Rate your peer's mastery of the success criterion (this is the *last* thing you do):

[ ] I can (still) graph linear equations.

0—DO NOT check that box	1—ALMOST check that box	2—CHECK that box
Many mathematical errors and/ or incomplete or unclear annotations	Few mathematical errors and/ or somewhat incomplete or unclear annotations	No mathematical errors and perfectly complete and clear annotations

[ ] I can approximate solutions to systems of equations by creating graphs.

0—DO NOT check that box	1—ALMOST check that box	2—CHECK that box

[ ] I can explain solutions to systems of equations in writing.

0—DO NOT check that box	1—ALMOST check that box	2—CHECK that box

DRAFT SOLUTION

ANNOTATIONS (author's and peer's)

REVISED SOLUTION

ANNOTATIONS (author only)

Figure 5.9

 This peer-assisted reflection task is available for download at resources.corwin.com/vlmathematics-6-8.

Teaching Takeaway

To provide the most amount of feedback to the greatest number of learners possible, incorporate student-to-student feedback and strategies for students' student-to-self feedback.

EFFECT SIZE FOR ASSESSMENT-CAPABLE VISIBLE LEARNERS = 1.33

Video 15
Feedback Through Peer-Assisted Reflection

https://resources.corwin.com/vlmathematics-6-8

Self-regulation feedback involves the learner self-monitoring his or her own progress toward a specific goal.

The PAR system provides students actionable feedback—often delivered by peers—that they can use to further take control of their own learning and develop into assessment-capable visible learners. The PAR cycle gives students the opportunity to compare and contrast: *This is what I used to be able to do; this is what I can do now. This is how I used to think about this problem; this is how I think about it now. This is what I used to know; this is what I know now.* In addition to these before-and-after snapshots, the feedback and annotation components of PARs can collect much of the connective tissue that bridged students from where they were to where they are. In other words, not only does growth as an outcome become blatant to students, but students become aware of their own growth process as well.

Process feedback supports making connections, use of multiple strategies, self-explanation, self-monitoring, self-questioning, and critical thinking. For example, Ms. Norris may ask a learner what strategies he or she used in making the decisions about percent increase or decrease and ask if a particular strategy worked well or if a different strategy may be more efficient. Rather than focusing solely on the correct answer regarding the relationship between an independent and a dependent variable, a teacher may ask a student, "What is your explanation for your answer?" The focus of process feedback is on the relationships between ideas, students' strategies for evaluating the reasonableness of an answer or solution, explicitly learning from mistakes, and helping the learner identify different strategies for addressing a task.

Like task feedback, process feedback should be specific and constructive and should support learners' pathways toward self-regulation feedback. That is, the feedback should deepen thinking, reasoning, explanations, and connections. Does the teacher prompt learners through strategic questioning related to the learning process? What appears to be wrong, and why? What approach or strategies did the learner use or apply to the task? What is an explanation for the answer, response, or solution? What are the relationships with other parts of the task? Watch Video 15 to see how co-author Joseph Assof conducts a PAR in his high school classroom.

Self-Regulation Feedback

Self-regulation feedback is the learner knowing what to do when she or he approaches a new and different problem, is stuck, or has to apply concepts and thinking in a new way. Learners who have reached a deep level of conceptual understanding and are armed with multiple strategies are equipped to self-regulate as they transfer their learning to more rigorous tasks. Highly proficient learners benefit from self-regulation feedback, although this is not the only type of feedback that is important to these learners. For example, when teachers detect a misconception or a gap in foundational or background learning, learners benefit from both task and process feedback in these situations. However, a majority of the feedback at this part of the learning process should be self-regulation through meta-cognition. The teacher's role in the feedback at this level is to ask questions to prompt further meta-cognition.

Eventually, learners practice meta-cognition independently through self-verbalization, self-questioning, and self-reflection. Ms. Norris recalls a student working diligently on the mastery task in Figure 5.1. Midway through the task, the learner stopped and began to erase his work, stating, "This answer does not make sense with the picture and I can't think of a scenario where my answer works. It must be wrong." Learners take personal ownership of their learning, which provides increased motivation and understanding. This is a well-documented finding in education research (e.g., National Research Council, 2000). The ability to think about your own thinking promotes learners' self-awareness, problem solving around the learning task, and understanding what they need to do to complete the task. To reiterate, learners know what to do, when they get stuck, when a new challenge arises, and when their teacher may not be available. This is self-regulation feedback.

> The ability to think about your own thinking promotes learners' self-awareness, problem solving around the learning task, and understanding what they need to do to complete the task.

> EFFECT SIZE FOR SELF-VERBALIZATION AND SELF-QUESTIONING = 0.55, AND SELF-REFLECTION = 0.75

Conclusion

Over the course of this book, we set out to portray the teaching of mathematics in the Visible Learning classroom. This brought together three elements of mathematics learning (conceptual understanding, procedural knowledge, and the application of concepts and thinking skills) with three phases of learning: surface, deep, and transfer (Figures 5.10 through 5.12).

Visible mathematics learning is an attainable goal when mathematics teachers *see* learning through the eyes of their students and students *see* themselves as their own mathematics teachers. Together, this type

MS. HALSTROM'S VISIBLE LEARNING IN THE MATHEMATICS CLASSROOM

Conceptual Understanding: the proportional relationship between the circumference and area of a circle.

Procedural Knowledge: the mathematical calculation of the circumference and area of a circle.

Application: using the circumference and area to calculate volumes and surface areas of cylinders.

Figure 5.10

MS. FERNANDEZ'S VISIBLE LEARNING IN THE MATHEMATICS CLASSROOM

Conceptual Understanding: a system of equations is a set of two or more equations with the same unknowns.

Procedural Knowledge: graphing linear equations is a means of solving systems of equations as intersections of equations signify their solutions.

Application: using systems of linear equations to make informed decisions about a real-world problem.

Figure 5.11

MR. SINGH'S VISIBLE LEARNING IN THE MATHEMATICS CLASSROOM

Conceptual Understanding: the role of positive and negative numbers in real-world contexts.

Procedural Knowledge: rules and patterns for adding integers.

Application: using integers to solve problems involving temperature comparisons and changes.

Figure 5.12

of learning environment develops assessment-capable visible learners. These learners can do the following:

1. Know their current level of mathematics learning.

2. Know where they are going next in mathematics and be confident to take on the challenge.

3. Select the most appropriate tools, problem-solving approaches, and skills to guide their learning.

4. Seek feedback and recognize errors are opportunities to enhance their mathematics learning.

5. Monitor their progress and adjust their mathematics learning.

6. Recognize their learning and support their peers in their own mathematics learning journey.

Teaching mathematics in the Visible Learning classroom demands as much from the teacher as from the learner. We have to create a learning environment that promotes clarity in learning, provides challenging mathematics tasks, checks for understanding, and enables a clear evaluation of mastery. We must know our impact on learning! Yes, there will be days that are better than others. Learning will be stronger with some content than other content. On the most successful days, celebrate the learning that your students do. On days when there is a less than desirable impact on student learning, stay focused on the main thing. We keep the main thing *the main thing* by recalibrating our mindframes about teaching and learning in the mathematics classroom. We can do this by asking ourselves these recalibrating questions:

1. What do I want my students to learn?

2. What evidence will convince me that they have learned it?

3. How will I check learners' understanding and progress?

4. What tasks will get my students to mastery?

5. How will I adjust the rigor of the tasks to meet the needs of all learners?

6. What resources do I need?

7. How will I manage the learning?

The classrooms of Ms. Halstrom, Ms. Fernandez, Mr. Singh, and Ms. Norris do just that, daily.

Final Reflection

Summarizing the content in this book, reflect on the following questions:

1. Using a specific standard or standards for an upcoming unit, describe what mastery would look like for that content.

2. How will you check for understanding as your learners progress toward mastery? How will these checks be different from your evaluation of their mastery of the standard or standards?

3. How do you plan to evaluate mastery of this particular content—task, test, or both?

4. Reflect on a recent mathematics task in your classroom. Using the definition and characteristics from this chapter, does it "qualify" as a challenging mathematics task?

5. Explain the role of feedback in supporting your learners' journey to mastery.

Appendix A

Effect Sizes

The Visible Learning research synthesizes findings from **1,800** meta-analyses of **80,000** studies involving **300** million students, into what works best in education.

STUDENT		ES
Prior knowledge and background		
Field independence	�	0.68
Non-standard dialect use	○	−0.29
Piagetian programs	●	1.28
Prior ability	●	0.94
Prior achievement	�	0.55
Relating creativity to achievement	�	0.40
Relations of high school to university achievement	�	0.60
Relations of high school achievement to career performance	●	0.38
Assessment-capable visible learners	●	1.33
Working memory strength	�	0.57
Beliefs, attitudes, and dispositions		
Attitude to content domains	●	0.35
Concentration/persistence/engagement	◑	0.56
Grit/incremental vs. entity thinking	●	0.25
Mindfulness	●	0.29
Morning vs. evening	◌	0.12
Perceived task value	◑	0.46
Positive ethnic self-identity	◌	0.12
Positive self-concept	◑	0.41
Self-efficacy	●	0.92
Stereotype threat	○	−0.33
Student personality attributes	●	0.26
Motivational approach, orientation		
Achieving motivation and approach	◑	0.44
Boredom	○	−0.49
Deep motivation and approach	◑	0.69
Depression	○	−0.36
Lack of stress	◌	0.17
Mastery goals	◌	0.06
Motivation	◑	0.42
Performance goals	○	−0.01
Reducing anxiety	◑	0.42
Surface motivation and approach	○	−0.11
Physical influences		
ADHD	○	−0.90
ADHD − treatment with drugs	●	0.32
Breastfeeding	◌	0.04
Deafness	○	−0.61
Exercise/relaxation	●	0.26
Gender on achievement	◌	0.08
Lack of illness	●	0.26
Lack of sleep	○	−0.05
Full compared to pre-term/low birth weight	◑	0.57
Relative age within a class	◑	0.45

CURRICULA		ES
Reading, writing, and the arts		
Comprehensive instructional programs for teachers	●	0.72
Comprehension programs	◑	0.47
Drama/arts programs	●	0.38
Exposure to reading	◑	0.43
Music programs	●	0.37
Phonics instruction	●	0.70
Repeated reading programs	●	0.75
Second/third chance programs	◑	0.53
Sentence combining programs	◌	0.15
Spelling programs	◑	0.58
Visual-perception programs	◑	0.55
Vocabulary programs	◑	0.62
Whole language approach	◌	0.06
Writing programs	◑	0.45
Math and sciences		
Manipulative materials on math	●	0.30
Mathematics programs	◑	0.59
Science programs	◑	0.48
Use of calculators	●	0.27
Other curricula programs		
Bilingual programs	●	0.36
Career interventions	●	0.38
Chess instruction	●	0.34
Conceptual change programs	●	0.99
Creativity programs	◑	0.62
Diversity courses	◌	0.09
Extra-curricula programs	●	0.20
Integrated curricula programs	◑	0.47
Juvenile delinquent programs	◌	0.12
Motivation/character programs	●	0.34
Outdoor/adventure programs	◑	0.43
Perceptual-motor programs	◌	0.08
Play programs	◑	0.50
Social skills programs	●	0.39
Tactile stimulation programs	◑	0.58

Access the complete and most recent versions of the influence chart at https://www.visiblelearningplus.com/content/research-john-hattie

HOME	ES
Family structure	
Adopted vs. non-adopted care	● 0.25
Engaged vs. disengaged fathers	● 0.20
Intact (two-parent) families	● 0.23
Other family structure	◐ 0.16
Home environment	
Corporal punishment in the home	○ −0.33
Early years' interventions	◉ 0.44
Home visiting	● 0.29
Moving between schools	○ −0.34
Parental autonomy support	◐ 0.15
Parental involvement	◉ 0.50
Parental military deployment	○ −0.16
Positive family/home dynamics	◉ 0.52
Television	○ −0.18
Family resources	
Family on welfare/state aid	○ −0.12
Non-immigrant background	◐ 0.01
Parental employment	◐ 0.03
Socio-economic status	◉ 0.52

SCHOOL	ES
Leadership	
Collective teacher efficacy	● 1.57
Principals/school leaders	● 0.32
School climate	● 0.32
School resourcing	
External accountability systems	● 0.31
Finances	● 0.21
Types of school	
Charter schools	◐ 0.09
Religious schools	● 0.24
Single-sex schools	◐ 0.08
Summer school	● 0.23
Summer vacation effect	○ −0.02
School compositional effects	
College halls of residence	◐ 0.05
Desegregation	● 0.28
Diverse student body	◐ 0.10
Middle schools' interventions	◐ 0.08
Out-of-school curricula experiences	● 0.26
School choice programs	◐ 0.12
School size (600–900 students at secondary)	◉ 0.43
Other school factors	
Counseling effects	● 0.35
Generalized school effects	◉ 0.48
Modifying school calendars/ timetables	◐ 0.09
Pre-school programs	● 0.28
Suspension/expelling students	○ −0.20

CLASSROOM	ES
Classroom composition effects	
Detracking	◐ 0.09
Mainstreaming/inclusion	● 0.27
Multi-grade/age classes	◐ 0.04
Open vs. traditional classrooms	◐ 0.01
Reducing class size	● 0.21
Retention (holding students back)	○ −0.32
Small group learning	◉ 0.47
Tracking/streaming	◐ 0.12
Within class grouping	◐ 0.18
School curricula for gifted students	
Ability grouping for gifted students	● 0.30
Acceleration programs	◉ 0.68
Enrichment programs	◉ 0.53
Classroom influences	
Background music	◐ 0.10
Behavioral intervention programs	◉ 0.62
Classroom management	● 0.35
Cognitive behavioral programs	● 0.29
Decreasing disruptive behavior	● 0.34
Mentoring	◐ 0.12
Positive peer influences	◉ 0.53
Strong classroom cohesion	◉ 0.44
Students feeling disliked	○ −0.19

TEACHER	ES
Teacher attributes	
Average teacher effects	● 0.32
Teacher clarity	● 0.75
Teacher credibility	● 0.90
Teacher estimates of achievement	● 1.29
Teacher expectations	◉ 0.43
Teacher personality attributes	◉ 0.23
Teacher performance pay	◐ 0.05
Teacher verbal ability	● 0.22
Teacher-student interactions	
Student rating of quality of teaching	◉ 0.50
Teachers not labeling students	◉ 0.61
Teacher-student relationships	◉ 0.52
Teacher education	
Initial teacher training programs	◐ 0.12
Micro-teaching/video review of lessons	● 0.88
Professional development programs	◉ 0.41
Teacher subject matter knowledge	◐ 0.11

Key for rating

● Potential to considerably accelerate student achievement

◉ Potential to accelerate student achievement

● Likely to have positive impact on student achievement

◐ Likely to have small positive impact on student achievement

○ Likely to have a negative impact on student achievement

ES Effect size calculated using Cohen's *d*

visible learning^plus

corwin.com/visiblelearning

The Visible Learning research synthesizes findings from **1,800** meta-analyses of **80,000** studies involving **300** million students, into what works best in education.

TEACHING: Focus on student learning strategies

	ES
Strategies emphasizing student meta-cognitive/self-regulated learning	
Elaboration and organization	0.75
Elaborative interrogation	0.42
Evaluation and reflection	0.75
Meta-cognitive strategies	0.60
Help seeking	0.72
Self-regulation strategies	0.52
Self-verbalization and self-questioning	0.55
Strategy monitoring	0.58
Transfer strategies	0.86
Student-focused interventions	
Aptitude/treatment interactions	0.19
Individualized instruction	0.23
Matching style of learning	0.31
Student-centered teaching	0.36
Student control over learning	0.02
Strategies emphasizing student perspectives in learning	
Peer tutoring	0.53
Volunteer tutors	0.26
Learning strategies	
Deliberate practice	0.79
Effort	0.77
Imagery	0.45
Interleaved practice	0.21
Mnemonics	0.76
Note taking	0.50
Outlining and transforming	0.66
Practice testing	0.54
Record keeping	0.52
Rehearsal and memorization	0.73
Spaced vs. mass practice	0.60
Strategy to integrate with prior knowledge	0.93
Study skills	0.46
Summarization	0.79
Teaching test taking and coaching	0.30
Time on task	0.49
Underlining and highlighting	0.50

TEACHING: Focus on teaching/instructional strategies

	ES
Strategies emphasizing learning intentions	
Appropriately challenging goals	0.59
Behavioral organizers	0.42
Clear goal intentions	0.48
Cognitive task analysis	1.29
Concept mapping	0.64
Goal commitment	0.40
Learning goals vs. no goals	0.68
Learning hierarchies-based approach	0.19
Planning and prediction	0.76
Setting standards for self-judgement	0.62
Strategies emphasizing success criteria	
Mastery learning	0.57
Worked examples	0.37
Strategies emphasizing feedback	
Classroom discussion	0.82
Different types of testing	0.12
Feedback	0.70
Providing formative evaluation	0.48
Questioning	0.48
Response to intervention	1.29
Teaching/instructional strategies	
Adjunct aids	0.32
Collaborative learning	0.34
Competitive vs. individualistic learning	0.24
Cooperative learning	0.40
Cooperative vs. competitive learning	0.53
Cooperative vs. individualistic learning	0.55
Direct/deliberate instruction	0.60
Discovery-based teaching	0.21
Explicit teaching strategies	0.57
Humor	0.04
Inductive teaching	0.44
Inquiry-based teaching	0.40
Jigsaw method	1.20
Philosophy in schools	0.43
Problem-based learning	0.26
Problem-solving teaching	0.68
Reciprocal teaching	0.74
Scaffolding	0.82
Teaching communication skills and strategies	0.43

Access the complete and most recent versions of the influence chart at https://www.visiblelearningplus.com/content/research-john-hattie

TEACHING: Focus on implementation method		ES
Implementations using technologies		
Clickers	●	0.22
Gaming/simulations	●	0.35
Information communications technology (ICT)	◉	0.47
Intelligent tutoring systems	◉	0.48
Interactive video methods	◉	0.54
Mobile phones	●	0.37
One-on-one laptops	○	0.16
Online and digital tools	●	0.29
Programmed instruction	●	0.23
Technology in distance education	○	0.01
Technology in mathematics	●	0.33
Technology in other subjects	◉	0.55
Technology in reading/literacy	●	0.29
Technology in science	●	0.23
Technology in small groups	●	0.21
Technology in writing	◉	0.42
Technology with college students	◉	0.42
Technology with elementary students	◉	0.44
Technology with high school students	●	0.30
Technology with learning needs students	◉	0.57
Use of PowerPoint	●	0.26
Visual/audio-visual methods	●	0.22
Web-based learning	○	0.18
Implementations using out-of-school learning		
After-school programs	◉	0.40
Distance education	○	0.13
Home-school programs	○	0.16
Homework	●	0.29
Service learning	◉	0.58
Implementations that emphasize school-wide teaching strategies		
Co- or team teaching	○	0.19
Interventions for students with learning needs	●	0.77
Student support programs – college	●	0.21
Teaching creative thinking	●	0.34
Whole-school improvement programs	●	0.28

Key for rating

● Potential to considerably accelerate student achievement

◉ Potential to accelerate student achievement

● Likely to have positive impact on student achievement

○ Likely to have small positive impact on student achievement

○ Likely to have a negative impact on student achievement

ES Effect size calculated using Cohen's *d*

Appendix B

Teaching for Clarity Planning Guide

Teaching for Clarity PLANNING GUIDE

ESTABLISHING PURPOSE

1 **What are the key content standards I will focus on in this lesson?**

2 **What are the learning intentions (the goal and *why* of learning, stated in student-friendly language) I will focus on in this lesson?**

Content:

Language:

Social:

3 When will I introduce and reinforce the learning intention(s) so that students understand it, see the relevance, connect it to previous learning, and can clearly communicate it themselves?

SUCCESS CRITERIA

4 What evidence shows that students have mastered the learning intention(s)? What criteria will I use?

I can statements:

5   How will I check students' understanding (assess learning) during instruction and make accommodations?

INSTRUCTION

6   What activities and tasks will move students forward in their learning?

7   What resources (materials and sentence frames) are needed?

8 How will I organize and facilitate the learning? What questions will I ask? How will I initiate closure?

Appendix C

Learning Intentions and Success Criteria Template

Learning Intentions	Conceptual Understanding	Procedural Knowledge	Application of Concepts and Thinking Skills
Unistructural (one idea)			
Multistructural (many ideas)			
Relational (related ideas)			
Extended abstract (extending ideas)			

Success Criteria	Conceptual Understanding	Procedural Knowledge	Application of Concepts and Thinking Skills
Unistructural (one idea)			
Multistructural (many ideas)			
Relational (related ideas)			
Extended abstract (extending ideas)			

 This template is available for download at resources.corwin.com/vlmathematics-6-8.

Appendix D

A Selection of International Mathematical Practice or Process Standards*

*Note that this is a nonexhaustive list of international mathematical practice/process standards as of June 2016. Because standards are often under review, you can look to your own state or country's individual documents to find the most up-to-date practice/process standards.

USA Common Core State Standards 8 Mathematical Practices[a]	USA Texas Essential Knowledge and Skills TEKS 7 Mathematical Practice Standards[b]	USA Virginia Mathematics 5 Standards of Learning[c]	International Baccalaureate 6 Assessment Objectives[d]	Hong Kong Key Learning Area 7 Generic Skills[e]	Singapore Mathematical Problem-Solving Processes[f]	Australian F-10 Mathematics Curriculum Key Ideas[g]
1. Make sense of problems and persevere in solving them.	A. Apply mathematics to problems arising in everyday life, society, and the workplace.	Mathematical problem solving	Knowledge and understanding	Collaboration skills	Reasoning, communications, and connections	Understanding
2. Reason abstractly and quantitatively.	B. Use a problem-solving model that incorporates analyzing given information, formulating a plan or strategy, determining a solution, justifying the solution, and evaluating the problem-solving process and the reasonableness of the solution.	Mathematical communication	Problem solving	Communication skills	Applications and modeling	Fluency
3. Construct viable arguments and critique the reasoning of others.		Mathematical reasoning	Communication and interpretation	Creativity	Thinking skills and heuristics	Problem solving
4. Use appropriate tools strategically.		Mathematical connection	Technology	Critical-thinking skills		Reasoning
5. Attend to precision.	C. Select tools, including real objects, manipulatives, paper and pencil, and technology as appropriate.	Mathematical representations	Reasoning	Information technology skills		
6. Look for and make use of structure.	D. Communicate mathematical ideas, reasoning, and their implications using multiple representations, including symbols, diagrams, graphs, and language as appropriate.		Inquiry approaches	Numeracy skills		
				Problem-solving skills		

(Continued)

(Continued)

USA Common Core State Standards 8 Mathematical Practices[a]	USA Texas Essential Knowledge and Skills TEKS 7 Mathematical Practice Standards[b]	USA Virginia Mathematics 5 Standards of Learning[c]	International Baccalaureate 6 Assessment Objectives[d]	Hong Kong Key Learning Area 7 Generic Skills[e]	Singapore Mathematical Problem-Solving Processes[f]	Australian F-10 Mathematics Curriculum Key Ideas[g]
7. Look for and express regularity in repeated reasoning.	E. Create and use representations to organize, record, and communicate mathematical ideas.					
8. Model with mathematics.	F. Analyze mathematical relationships to connect and communicate mathematical ideas. G. Display, explain, and justify mathematical ideas and arguments using precise mathematical language in written or oral communication.					

[a]Retrieved June 22, 2016, from http://www.corestandards.org/Math/Practice/.

[b]Retrieved June 22, 2016, from http://ritter.tea.state.tx.us/rules/tac/chapter111/ch111a.html.

[c]Retrieved June 22, 2016, from http://www.doe.virginia.gov/testing/sol/standards_docs/mathematics/2009/stds_math.pdf.

[d]Retrieved June 22, 2016, from http://www.ibo.org/globalassets/publications/recognition/5_mathsl.pdf.

[e]Retrieved June 22, 2016, from http://www.edb.gov.hk/attachment/en/curriculum-development/kla/ma/curr/Math_CAGuide_e_2015.pdf.

[f]Retrieved June 22, 2016, from https://www.moe.gov.sg/docs/default-source/document/education/syllabuses/sciences/files/mathematics-syllabus-(primary-1-to-4).pdf.

[g]Retrieved June 22, 2016, from http://www.australiancurriculum.edu.au/mathematics/curriculum/f-10?layout=1.

Source: Standards for Mathematical Practice, CCSSO.

References

American Psychological Association, Coalition for Psychology in Schools and Education. (2015). *Top 20 principles from psychology for preK–12 teaching and learning.* Retrieved from http://www.apa.org/ed/schools/cpse/top-twenty-principles.pdf

Antonetti, J., & Garver, J. (2015). *17,000 classroom visits can't be wrong.* Alexandria, VA: Association for Supervision and Curriculum Development.

Biggs, J. B., & Collis, K. F. (1982). *Evaluating the quality of learning: The SOLO taxonomy (structure of the observed learning outcome).* New York, NY: Academic Press.

Boaler, J. (2015). *What's math got to do with it? How teachers and parents can transform mathematics learning and inspire success* (Rev. ed.). New York, NY: Penguin.

Boaler, J. (2016). *Mathematical mindsets.* New York, NY: Jossey-Bass.

Boaler, J., & Humpreys, C. (2005). *Connecting mathematical ideas: Middle school video cases to support teaching and learning.* Portsmouth, NH: Heinemann.

Cole, M., John-Steiner, V., Scribner, S., & Souberman, E. (Eds.). (1978). *Mind in society: The development of higher psychological processes.* L. S. Vygotsky. Oxford, England: Harvard University Press.

Fennell, F. S., Kobett, B. M., & Wray, J. A. (2017). *The formative 5: Everyday assessment techniques for every math classroom.* Thousand Oaks, CA: Corwin.

Fisher, D., & Frey, N. (2008). Homework and the gradual release of responsibility: Making "responsibility" possible. *English Journal, 98*(2), 40–45.

Frey, N., Hattie, J., & Fisher, D. (2018). *Developing assessment-capable visible learners.* Thousand Oaks, CA: Corwin.

Guskey, T. R. (2014). *On your mark: Challenging the conventions of grading and reporting.* Bloomington, IN: Solution Tree.

Hattie, J. (2009). *Visible learning: A synthesis of over 800 meta-analyses relating to achievement.* New York, NY: Routledge.

Hattie, J., Fisher, D., Frey, N., Gojak, L. M., Moore, S. D., & Mellman, W. (2017). *Visible learning for mathematics: What works best to optimize student learning.* Thousand Oaks, CA: Corwin.

Hattie, J., & Timperley, H. (2007). The power of feedback. *Review of Educational Research, 77*(1), 81–112.

Hattie, J., & Zierer, K. (2018). *Ten mindframes for visible learning: Teaching for success.* New York, NY: Routledge.

Herbel-Eisenmann, B. A., & Breyfogle, M. L. (2005). Questioning our patterns of questioning. *Mathematics Teaching in the Middle School, 10*(9), 484–489.

Hook, P., & Mills, J. (2011). *SOLO taxonomy: A guide for schools. Book 1.* Laughton, United Kingdom: Essential Resources.

Linn, R. L., & Gronlund, N. E. (2000). *Measurement and assessment in teaching* (8th ed.). Upper Saddle River, NJ: Merrill Prentice Hall.

National Council of Teachers of Mathematics. (2014). *Principles to actions: Ensuring mathematical success for all.* Reston, VA: Author.

National Governors Association Center for Best Practices, Council of Chief State School Officers. (2010). *Common Core State Standards for Mathematics.* Washington, DC: Author.

National Research Council. (2000). *How people learn: Brain, mind, experience, and school: Expanded edition.* Washington, DC: The National Academies Press. Retrieved from https://doi.org/10.17226/9853

Neuschwander, C., & Geehan, W. (1997). *Sir cumference and the first round table.* Watertown, MA: Charlesbridge Publishing.

Reinholz, D. L. (2015). Peer-assisted reflection: A design-based intervention for improving success in calculus. *International Journal of Research in Undergraduate Mathematics Education, 1*(2), 234–267.

Schlechty, P. C. (2002). *Working on the work: An action plan for teachers, principals, and superintendents.* San Francisco, CA: Jossey-Bass.

Shell Center for Mathematical Education. (2015). *Using positive and negative numbers in context.* Retrieved from http://map.mathshell.org/lessons.php?unit=7105&collection=8

Smith, M. S., & Stein, M. K. (2011). *Five practices for orchestrating productive mathematics discussions.* Reston, VA: National Council of Teachers of Mathematics.

Usiskin, Z. (2014). Unpacking mathematical understanding in the Common Core (2012). In B. J. Reys & R. E. Reys (Eds.), *We need another revolution: Five decades of mathematics curriculum papers* (pp. 212–224). Reston, VA: National Council of Teachers of Mathematics.

Virginia Department of Education. (2016). *Mathematics Standards of Learning for Virginia Public Schools.* Retrieved from http://www.doe.virginia.gov/testing/sol/standards_docs/mathematics/2016/index.shtml

Wolf, N. B. (2015). *Modeling with mathematics: Authentic problem solving in middle school.* Portsmouth, NH: Heinemann Publishing.

Wood, T. (1998). Alternative patterns of communication in mathematics classes: Funneling or focusing? In H. Steinbring, M. G. Bartolini Bussi, & A. Sierpinska (Eds.), *Language and communication in the mathematics classroom* (pp. 167–178). Reston, VA: National Council of Teachers of Mathematics.

Youcubed. (2014). *Youcubed.* Retrieved from https://www.youcubed.org/

Index

)

3 Ways to get started with Visible Learning^plus®

The power of the **Visible Learning^plus School Impact Process**—based on Professor John Hattie's research—lies in evidence-based cycles of inquiry and action that help you align your strategic priorities to the factors that accelerate student achievement.

1

Attend an Event

Discover the core concepts of the Visible Learning™ research at a local event led by one of our world-class presenters.

2

Measure Your Baseline

Determine the extent to which high-impact practices are present in your school. A certified Visible Learning^plus consultant will collect your data and present an unbiased, written baseline report to help you track progress and measure growth.

3

Build a Foundation

Develop a cycle of inquiry and knowledge building into your school's professional learning planning process so that your time, energy, and resources are focused on what is having the greatest impact on your students' learning.

VLN199E1

Learn more at visiblelearningplus.com

CORWIN

All students should have the opportunity to be successful!

Visible Learning^plus is based on one simple belief: Every student should experience at least one year's growth over the course of one school year. Visible Learning^plus translates the groundbreaking Visible Learning research by professor John Hattie into a practical model of inquiry and evaluation. Bring Visible Learning to your daily classroom practice with these additional resources across mathematics, literacy, and science.

John Hattie, Douglas Fisher, Nancy Frey, Linda M. Gojak, Sara Delano Moore, and William Mellman

Discover the right mathematics strategy to use at each learning phase so all students demonstrate more than a year's worth of learning per school year.

Grades K–2 and 3–5 coming in 2019!

John Almarode, Douglas Fisher, Joseph Assof, Sara Delano Moore, John Hattie, and Nancy Frey

Leverage the most effective teaching practices at the most effective time to meet the surface, deep, and transfer learning needs of every mathematics student.

Douglas Fisher, Nancy Frey, and John Hattie

Ensure students demonstrate more than a year's worth of learning during a school year by implementing the right literacy practice at the right moment.

Douglas Fisher, Nancy Frey, John Hattie, and Marisol Thayre

High-impact strategies to use for all you teach—all in one place. Deliver sustained, comprehensive literacy experiences to K–12 learners each day.

Nancy Frey, John Hattie, and Douglas Fisher

Imagine students who understand their educational goals and monitor their progress. This illuminating book focuses on self-assessment as a springboard for markedly higher levels of student achievement.

John Almarode, Douglas Fisher, Nancy Frey, and John Hattie

Inquiry, laboratory, project-based learning, discovery learning? The authors reveal that it's not which strategy, but when, and plot a vital K–12 framework for choosing the right approach at the right time.

corwin.com

CORWIN

N18AD7

Let us know what you think!

Did the information in this book resonate with you? We're hoping you'll continue to support this book's journey to reaching teachers and having the ultimate impact in the classroom. Here are a few ways you can do that:

> > > **JOIN** the conversation! Share your comments, participate in an online book study, or post a picture of yourself with the book on social media using **#VLClassroom**.

> > > **PROVIDE** your expert review of *Teaching Mathematics in the Visible Learning Classroom, Grades 6–8* on Amazon.

> > > **LEAD** or join a book study in your school or team to share ideas on how to bring the concepts presented in the book to life.

> > > **FOLLOW** our Corwin in the Classroom Facebook page and share your Visible Learning strategies in the mathematics classroom using **#VLClassroom**.

> > > **RECOMMEND** this book for your Professional Learning Community activities.

> > > **SUGGEST** this book to teacher educators.

Be sure to stay up-to-date on all things Corwin by following us on social media:
Facebook: www.facebook.com/corwinclassroom
Instagram: www.instagram.com/corwin_press, @corwin_press
Twitter: twitter.com/CorwinPress, @CorwinPress
Pinterest: www.pinterest.com/corwinpress/pins

www.corwin.com

CORWIN
A SAGE Publishing Company

Helping educators make the greatest impact

CORWIN HAS ONE MISSION: to enhance education through intentional professional learning.

We build long-term relationships with our authors, educators, clients, and associations who partner with us to develop and continuously improve the best evidence-based practices that establish and support lifelong learning.